MENE, MENE, TEKEL UPHARSIN

Thou art weighed in the balances,
and art found wanting.
Daniel 5:27

PROPHETIC POETRY FOR THESE PERILOUS END-TIMES

*4 They drank wine, and praised the gods of gold, and of
silver, of brass, of iron, of wood, and of stone.
5 In the same hour came forth fingers of a man's hand,
and wrote over against the candlestick upon
the plaister of the wall of the king's palace:
and the king saw the part of the hand that wrote.
6 Then the king's countenance was changed, and his
thoughts troubled him, so that the joints of his loins were
loosed, and his knees smote one against another. ...*

*24 Then was the part of the hand sent from him;
and this writing was written.
25 And this [is] the writing that was written,*
MENE, MENE, TEKEL, UPHARSIN.

Daniel 5:4-6, 24-25 KJV

MENE, MENE, TEKEL, UPHAR

Thou art weighed in the balances,
and art found wanting.
Daniel 5:27

PROPHETIC POETRY FOR THESE PERILOUS END-TIMES

by Marcella Burnes

BOLD TRUTH
PUBLISHING

A BOLD TRUTH Publication
Christian Literature & Artwork

MENE, MENE, TEKEL, UPHARS
Copyright © 2019 Marcella Burnes
ISBN 13: 978-1-949993-01-1

First Edition

BOLD TRUTH PUBLISHING
(Christian Literature & Artwork)
606 West 41st, Ste. 4
Sand Springs, Oklahoma 74063
www.BoldTruthPublishing.com

Available from Amazon.com and other retail outlets.
Orders by U.S. trade bookstores and wholesalers.
Email: *boldtruthbooks@yahoo.com*

Quantity sales special discounts are available on quantity purchases by corporations, associations, and others. For details, contact the publisher at the address above.

Artwork, formatting and overall design by Aaron Jones.

Cover photograph used by permission.

Printed in the USA.
02 19   10 9 8 7 6 5 4 3 2 1

Permissions

Permissions

Contents

Contents

Preface

We have never before in the history of man had the ability to comprehend the establishment of the fetal heartbeat to the exact science we know today. The advancement of technology have given us proof beyond a shadow of doubt, a fetal HEARTBEAT is detected at 22 days of (conception) life. THIS is being plainly shown to mankind. We have assumed in our arrogance and smugness that we know more than our Creator. The beginning of a human (spirit, soul and body) starts at the moment of conception. This is GOD'S WORD on the matter. Science is *constantly* discovering new facts that back up THE WORD OF GOD. Tomorrow may be the discovery of a cure for a cancer for all we know, (assuming we *don't* abort that answer)

We have lied to ourselves, and accepted the lies of a human sacrifice machine fueled by evil desire of self, convenience, and monetary gain.

A Wise, Holy, and Just GOD is exposing truth

We erroneously assumed a baby is a mere mass of tissue until birth. The case has already come before the courts of the universe and been deemed—MURDER.

The fear of a HOLY GOD has been shoved aside in America. The holocaustic cries of MILLIONS of *murdered innocent babies* has been shoved in GOD'S FACE for a generation plus.

GOD HIMSELF is making absolute certain that HIS case

Preface

against abortion (Roe v Wade) is being presented to man. GOD HIMSELF as the great judge, the jury, the defender, the prosecutor, and executioner of justice has presented HIS case to mankind. HE is about to render *judgement*.

The statue of the *'scales of justice'* sets on the desk of most of our attorneys and judges today. This is supposed be a reminder of the delicate balance that must be maintained on these scales. Mercy and justice, hand in hand; they must balance.

When the last drop of innocent blood drips onto the scales of justice and it tips awry a HOLY, JUST AND RIGHTEOUS GOD must render justice; because, it is HIS nature, HE is just—HE cannot lie.

This book is HIS case and HIS warning.

The prophesying of the North Section to America resounds with a terrifying and chilling warning to our nation. The courts have convened and the verdict has already been rendered and the punishment is prepared. Just as Jonah was sent to Ninevah to proclaim repentance and warn of judgement that was about to transpire; so also, this book has been sent. I pray that like Ninevah, America turns from our wickedness and repents before a HOLY GOD.

REPENTANCE OF ABORTION IN THIS NATION, IT MUST CEASE ALTOGETHER.

Acknowledgments

To my Heavenly Father I give all the glory honor and praise.
To His Son for His eternal salvation mercy and grace, to
the Holy Spirit for his gracious patience to me
GREAT IS THY FAITHFULNESS.

To my publisher and friend,
Aaron Jones and his family
for the many, many, hours of listening,
encouraging and praying me through this book.
I can only say thank you for NOT aborting this author
or this project in the third trimester of its completion.

To my Aunt Berniece Guest,
great is thy reward for your faithfulness.
I love you!

To Wanda, Rebecca, Lori, Ginny
and the many others who prayed and stood with me.
From the depths of my heart,
Thank you!

In memory of
one of the bravest girls I ever knew,
my daughter,
Missy Danielle Burnes
(Feb. 10, 1975 – Oct. 21, 2018)
who chose life for her three sons
in the face of all the odds.

Acknowledgements

Introduction

Mene, Mene, Tekel, Upharsin is a 'Warning' Word the Lord has given me over America for right now.

In the Old Testament, Book of Daniel Chapter 5 King Belshazzar had taken the holy things of God from His Temple. He used them for a profane drunken party. He also began to praise the gods of gold, silver, iron, wood, and stone; so much like America today. I say we have so overstepped and out-stripped the sins of Belshazzar; in the final analysis, America makes that historic account look like a picnic.

Consider, the blood of the [60 million plus] innocent babies that is on our hands since the 1973 court case of 'Roe vs. Wade' and the legalization of abortion. These aborted baby (parts) are sold for everything from expensive beauty products (collagen), advancements in medical science, and even experimental food production. Then, as abhorrent as this all seems, what's left is deemed medical waste and is thrown into landfills; these precious lives are not even honored with—a proper burial.

God's Word says, before I formed you in the belly (the womb), I knew you. (Je 1:5) We sacrifice our own children to the 'gods' of convenience and money, all on the altar of the 'god' of selfishness. Abortion is murder, no matter what you believe. Our rights, a woman's right, we cry when in all actuality it is just *the god of self* we are wholly serving.

What I am writing here is not a question of our rights. It

is not an open forum discussion. It is the truth, according to the [inerrant] Word of God—abortion is murder!

In 1973 The Supreme Court landmark decision of Roe vs. Wade came into existence. I was [17 years old] and graduating high school that year.

That year, I participated in and experienced one of the most heinous crimes to ever be perpetrated on humanity—I had an abortion.

Now at my age, looking back, this is a staggering, almost overwhelming thought to me. I was young, uneducated, impoverished, scared and alone (unwed); and even though, all of these described my situation at the time, none excuse the action. At no time before or after did I ever consider this a correct moral decision—my conscious knew better. But still, against God, that child, and my conscious I went through with an action never to be forgotten and always to be regretted.

After coming to know The Lord in salvation, I have experienced much prayer and ministry in this area of my life. Through this I have received total forgiveness. There is absolutely no sin Jesus does not forgive; however, the sin of abortion not only kills the child, but also scars the mother—in my case that scar was deep and painful. But, praise be to Jesus, He has healed me completely. And I know I will see my child one day in Heaven, in a much anticipated and glorious reunion.

Introduction

Fast forward to 2018, sitting in a church service in my small-town church, with the song 'Lay It All Down' playing. The Lord spoke to me "what's in your alabaster box?" Wow! He began to ask me to open and pour out to the world this costly perfume. My sin? Expose to the world? Oh No. Oh yes, how can I not? Thus began, my journey to write about and expose the Abortion Industry and The Laws God has given us about *'the shedding of innocent blood'*! Just one, I pray is saved through my testimony? Yes, and no! I pray it saves all, or I pray it be used as an instrument to overturn this evil ruling of the land—Roe vs. Wade; it must fall!

January 2018, Pastor John Kilpatrick prophesied over the nation (*see youtube "Words for 2018 and beyond" by John Kilpatrick) This is a 30 minute segment. I encourage everyone to watch. In this prophecy, Pastor Kilpatrick speaks of how The Lord in this year will interrupt, break in and let HIS MIND be known. This has happened to me. God begin to wake me in the early morning hours and speak to me; HE said to prophesy to America, the North, South, East and the West. I wrote what I heard and later watched as many of these prophecies came to pass. Some in my personal life, some in my local area, others on the national scene, and then, some have not yet transpired. Many of these prophecies [but not all] are published here. As I questioned The Lord on what I was hearing, I asked for confirmation. The Lord began to confirm His spoken Word to me with His written Word. Many of these Scripture references I use throughout the book.

Introduction

One of the words in Pastor Kilpatrick's prophecy states: *"The land is in chaos and must be requited because of the shedding of innocent blood."*

This single prophecy and statement has been, and is being played out before our very eyes.

The fingers of The Lord Almighty appeared on the wall and wrote: *"MENE MENE TEKEL UPHARSIN"*

Even in King Belshazzar's rebellious drunken stupor the fear of The Lord overcame him causing his knees to literally knock together.

Then godly counsel of the day was sought, and the handwriting deciphered:

- *Mene Mene*—means God has numbered the days of your kingdom and put an end to it.
- *Tekel*—You have been weighed on the scales of righteousness and found deficient.
- *Upharsin*—Your kingdom has been divided and given to the Medes and Persians.

Literally: *"Numbered, numbered, weighed and divided"*

Sincerely,
Marcella Burnes

∽

December, 2018
MIDNIGHT HOUR

I awake in the midnight hour: sometimes later
but under HIS power
HE tells me words to say
Sometimes visions;
I try to obey
Sleep wiped from my eyes
HIS WORD I never want to despise!
Really it comes to this
I write what I hear
Meanings not always clear.
Prophets of old were called to obey
Not really popular; same as today
A pleasant word much is not
But as always begins at the top.
Judgement begins at the house of GOD
This is meant for all to trod.
Rebellion rings across the land
Repentance sings from HIS hand
Glory, glory, glory I hear
When the fear of GOD does draw near!
Wash thy hands and thy heart
From this sin of abortion
Depart—dare ye not obey?
MY HAND of justice swings this way.

Introduction

SOUTH

MENE, MENE, TEKEL, UPHARSIN

~

THE MOTHER SHIPTON PROPHECY

The following excerpt is from a prophecy from Mother Ursula Shipton (1488-1571). Mother Shipton was burned at the stake, accused of being a witch, but in truth—she was a Prophetess of God way ahead of her time.

The women shall adopt a craze
To dress like men, and trousers wear
And to cut off their locks of hair
They'll ride astride with brazen brow
As witches do on broomstick now.
And roaring [1]monsters with man atop
Does seem to eat the verdant crop
And men shall [2]fly as birds do now
And give [3]away the horse and plough.
There'll be a sign for all to see
Be sure that it will certain be.
Then love shall die and [4]marriage cease
And nations wane as babes [5]decrease
And wives shall fondle cats and dogs
And men live much the same as [6]hogs.
In [7]nineteen hundred and twenty six
Build houses light of straw and sticks.
For then shall mighty [8]wars be planned
And fire and sword shall sweep the land.
When pictures [9]seem alive with movements free
When boats like fishes swim [10]beneath the sea,

When men like birds shall scour the sky
Then half the world, deep drenched in blood shall die.
For those who live the [11]century through
In fear and trembling this shall do.
Flee to the mountains and the [12]dens
To bog and forest and wild fens.
For storms will [13]rage and oceans roar
When Gabriel [14]stands on sea and shore
And as he blows his wondrous [15]horn
Old worlds die and [16]new be born.

[1]*Harvesting Combines*
[2]*Airplanes and jet aircraft*
[3]*Modern farming equipment (tractors, loaders, etc.)*
[4]*Greater than 2 out of every 3 marriages ends in divorce.*
[5]*Abortion, decline in child births as selfish ambition rises.*
[6]*Living for the flesh; hog—unclean animal*
[7]*The industrial age, 40 hour work week began*
[8]*World War 1 and 2, Korea, Vietnam, etc.*
[9]*T.V. and motion pictures*
[10]*Modern submarines*
[11]*1900-2000*
[12]*Survivalist and storm and bomb shelters*
[13]*Luke 21:25*
[14]*Revelation 10:1-6*
[15]*The Last Trump*
[16]*Millennium?*

~

February 12 2018
MEXICO, LOOK TO THE SOUTH
{Prophetic over U.S.}

Mexico, look to the South
Many trapped without
Precious are these to me
Barriers rock hard
Willing many to see
Scrabble, rabble
A deference, racing time, ticking clock
Hurrying before they turn the lock
Just about to overcome
They don't make it, they must run
Just about a bugle's call on the wall
Those who have been before will go again
Lining up believers like flaming arrows,
I will shoot them in
A Damascus Road, sign of weakness?
Paul never dreamed,
Sharing the Gospel, will be a new thing.

~

SHALL WE OBTAIN ONLY GOOD

You take the good with the bad

The glad with the sad
Then you be grateful for what you had
In other words
Shall we obtain only good from
THE HAND OF THE LORD

~

February 2018
DANGEROUS TIMES

Dangerous times are ahead
For THE SPIRIT OF THE LORD hath said
Leprosy shall rise [1]again
For this is a symbol of sin
The beginning from the end
Shall be told over and over again
Dead men's lies, bones a float
Altar calls, what she wrote
Repentance for MY sheep
Christening them as they weep
Altar calls, altar calls
Trumpet blast for them all
Belonging not to just a few
None shall you refuse

[1]*Leprosy is on the rise, reported in news, spreading through Armadillos prevalent in Florida*

~

March 15, 2018
WRITING ON THE WALLS
{Prophetic for Spring}

Bathroom walls will appear
With verses clear
Iniquity and sin
With blood stains on them
A chance to repent will be given to all
Oceans of love and mercy will fall
Graphic appearances of MY verse
Through the arts I will rehearse
John 3:16 .... shall be seen
On sidewalks in chalk; marbles will talk
Let the games begin, as I usher spring in.
Zip not the lips of MY babes
For I shall cause them to behave
With joy of a holy wave
Opposing sin, they shall be brave!!!

~

March 12, 2018
EVERYTHING CHANGES

Everything changes, our life rearranges
Nothing stays the same

Winners lose, losers win
Game changes
Stand not in sin
Obey THE LORD at all cost
Forgive a lot, forget not
Love covers a multitude of sin.
Be not afraid
Wash it not thin.

~

February 21, 2018
MY FRONT GATE IS OPEN

My front gate is open,
The porch light is on;
Return to a place safe and warm.
There is bread on the table,
And a good place to sleep.
Calling all sinners
To come home to eat.

~

April 17, 2018
A BATTLE CRY

A Hymn
Begin to worship

Praises bring THE SPIRIT in.
A bugle call reveille
[Stand tall],
JESUS is about to begin.
Rejection abounds

Of a ruling that's found,
Deplorable in HIS EYES—
HE does despise.

~

Winter, 2018
MUCK AND MIRE

Anger, envy, and strife
Corralled by THE GOOD SHEPHERD;
We begin in the herd.
When we do not listen
We wander astray from THE WORD.

Anger, jealousy, hatred, and strife
Begins in our heart—
Comes to steal our lives

Faith comes by hearing.
When we harden our hearts,
Dampen GOD'S SPIRIT and
Push ourselves apart.

We give place to the devil,

And wander astray
When we don't obey.

Believers can enjoy
The peace from within.
As The Church was before;
So now, it shall be again.

∾

April 2018
EPHESIANS' CHAPTER

Ephesians' chapter:
A trumpet call,
A final chapter.
Pray for order,
What 'I AM' is after.
"Holy, holy, holy"
Lies these cries.
Justice demands mercy rise.
A beginning of the end,
A blocked rebellion;
We do win!
A kick boxer's stance?
A victory dance?
A strangled choke hold?
Lover's lance—
A brand new chance.

~

July, 2018
A NEW DANCE

History repeats itself.
This time a new dance;
Retributions chance.
An army arising showered in MY love,
Will break history's shedding of more *innocent blood*.
Be still and know of this flood,
I will stop the enemy's chance,
I will break the lance of the abortion dance.

~

September 20, 2018
MY FINGERS FLY

My fingers fly thru the pages,
As I sense GOD moves closer to rages.
Sifted like wheat, blast from HIS breath,
We will eat.
Stubble burnt away,
As we laxly pray.
Genes dormant lay filled with righteous indignation;
Fueled by the enemy as he cages, kills and burns
Our children upon Baal's urn.
Sacrificial Lamb? That's what is—I AM.

No longer on the Cross,
He PAID IN FULL, the cost.
Defeated foe you will go!
In jeopardy, the will,
Of a large factory, *a mill.*
Not of the puppy sort,
But of humans, lives short.
Cracked open at half start,
Zero numbered by a cold heart.
Pulled from the womb, lives shortened, no room
At the inn, no place to lay, no manger, no hay;
In the short, let's abort
No pulling at *heart strings,*
Cast aside, it's only a thing.
Crowding closer JESUS retrieves this insane scene.
Believe me when GOD said,
"Morbidity rate at a full plate
My anger, it's now—too late."

～

March 7, 2018
GENDER ISSUE

Gender issue?
A woman's choice?
Lies, in the wait
A boy or girl did you create?

Clinging to old fashioned beliefs

Raising spirits of relief.
When THE LORD comes again,
What will HE find in our hand?

Old fashioned beliefs, have we birthed
About GOD'S creation on this Earth.

What sex did I get?
Son or daughter?
You say yet?

Open the diaper,
And you will see
What GOD intended you to be.
Our children are being taught from birth,
To reject themselves—it is a curse.

Rise up strong!
Right the wrong!
Humility is all it takes.
—Repent!—
I'll the curse break!

~

January 2018
A NEW PAGE
{After church shooting in Texas in Nov. 2017}

Killed our anger burns
Still, alive we have learned

Overcomers shot in rage
Soon dies down after becoming front page
Hear the news:
Before we finish crying the blues
Believers see a new page
Beginning with all the rage
Guns heavy we will tote
For peace to promote
Casting suspicious fear
For all who draws near
Know this says THE LORD
Obey MY WORD, don't abhor!
A brand new life I feel in me
Believers know this is from HIS tree
A shaking has already begun
Get yourself ready—*run Forest, run!*

～

June 8, 2018

UPDATED UNIONS

Updated unions I despise,
Creating havoc in MY eyes.
Bring to Capital Hill the bill to kill
Homosexual thrill.
Violation of MY ordinance,
Precedes official court announce:
Definition of a union.

Godly choice, I rejoice,
Matrimony for two again.
Species brave and bold,
Woman and man it was told.

~

April 24, 2018
A WAR ZONE

A war zone, a war zone
A capturing battlefields a blazing
No more lazing
A shot in the dark it will now start
Let all proclaim
Prepare the battle from the smallest to the lame
[1]Rivers of blood I will purge
Forging ahead, moving my herd.

[1]*As I write, there are currently several locations, i.e., France, Indonesia, and Russia; where rivers and streams are 'supernaturally' turning blood red.*

~

ORGAN-IZED CRIME

Organ-ized Crime
Selling babies' *body parts* one at a time
Every time we hear these stories

We turn our head, not believing the gory
-Details -
Entrails spilled upon the table
Brains, hearts and blood
Sold for money love
These stories are not fabled
Evil beyond belief
GOD is arising
HE now brings relief!

~

April 24, 2018
OPEN LITTLE EYES
{Prophetic}

A righteous FATHER
Calls to all
Put down thy food
Hear MY call
Listen to MY SPIRIT WIND
Changes
Running just begin
Open up thy V cart
Matrix makes a mark
Second place yet relies
Open little eyes
Suckling children
Hear the cry

Open birth canal
Wonder I

~

March 30, 2018
SINK OR SWIM
{Prophetic}

Dutch Sheets and all of them
Are trying to tell us sink or swim
But I hear them tell *the old, old story*
Bout ME
How I come from glory
Joined hands together to pray
Washed in MY blood
Stay in MY way
Obey grace generally speaking
Run the race GOD is sweeping
Kentuckians are calling for reform
Allowing prayer moving across the nation
Movement of MY SPIRIT reborn
Ocean waves come crashing
Obeying JESUS a wall-bashing
Breaking on MY SPIRIT WIND
Movement about to bend
Language at hand
Let prayer rule in this land
Let prayer begin again

~

April 1, 2018

A FOOL'S WAY ON FOOL'S DAY

As I am writing, I heard The Father and the following conversation in the spirit.

[THE FATHER] *"To not obey?*
Listen to what I say,
Move, obey.
Ushered from above,
Spoilt rebellion breaks through love
From under
Heavy thunder, crashing skies;
Hearing lots of children's cries.
Running quickly open eyes,
Oh, MY daughter don't despise.
Children, children
I hear their cries,
"Mama spare me please, break not my bones!"'

I hear from these
[THE UNBORN] *"These needles are coming close to kill me!"*
—A horrible, horrible, horrid sin!
[THE FATHER] *"I'M about to stop them."*

From nail scarred hands,
I still hear that cry:
[JESUS] *"FATHER forgive them,*
They know not why."

[THE FATHER] *"About face I must turn*
A SAVIOR'S blood, rescues its own.

[THE FATHER] *"But this is building to a boiling point,*
Lucifer wants every cartilage and joint.
Demons shout and cry:
I'm thirsty for blood—perpetuate the lie.

[THE FATHER] *"Repentance Church,*
Do you see the need?
It's something I'M expecting of—thee.
A battering weapon,
A battle cry.
Overcome the enemy,
Expose the lie!"

❧

YOU HAD A CHOICE

JESUS, JESUS,
You had a choice.
To die on that tree, YOU did not rejoice.

To sacrifice a SAVIOR'S LIFE
YOU did some praying
YOU had to think twice
For the joy set before YOU
YOU paid the price
YOU beat the devil
But YOU sacrificed.

To overcome him, YOU had to decide
Obedience to death to die.

A miracle we did see
When your will was laid down in *Gethsemane*
For the joy set before YOU
YOU counted the cost
YOU knew disobedience
To humanity would be lost

But that was not why YOU chose to obey
For I believe it was to hear THE FATHER say
Well done MY SON
Enter your reward today.

∾

ELOHIM AND EL SHADDAI
{Prophetic}

Watching over us with *single eye*
Perverseness shall not stand
Poverty or lack not part of GOD'S plan
Business endeavors
Ideas that are clever
Rewards are for the redeemed
Who have meet the requirements of EL-OHIM
THE VOICE OF EL-SHADDAI
Shall be lifted up on high
JESUS stands before the throne

Proving and knowing HIS own
Devouring all who would dare stand
United together against GOD'S PLAN.

~

A PRISONER'S YELL
{Prophetic}

A prisoner's yell
Revealing Hell
Bound by addictions
Releasing afflictions
Prisoners chains
I'M breaking the reigns
A list begins
Hear MY glory winds
Chains rattle
Break fall
To all prisoners I call
Dare to free thee
Yes—you will see!
Gaining ground in a war
Requires strict obedience.
Don't abhor

~

February 12, 2018
A BREAKTHROUGH—HEALINGS
{Prophetic}

Cerebral Palsy
A medical *breakthrough* from within
Cancer, redeemed,
Open healing like we've never seen
Darkness rebuked from many without
Cringing spirits moving out
Shut doors for a season
Flying open without reason

~

January, 2018
HOMELESS
{In memory of Kristal Friel}

Homeless
They are vanishing before our eyes into thin air
Right the wrong
"Christian"
Do you care?
Needless suffering on our streets
Homeless dying on corners that we meet.

In my home
The addict I despise
Hating while she lies
Bound by chains of addiction
Living hopeless with the friction
Wanting freedom all the while
Blocking help, like a child.
I'm hungry, they do cry
Lonely, scared, tired, helpless they die.

"Christians!"
Marching on Calvary's road
Staunch believers of THE WORD
Paths cross in the streets
Will you their needs meet?
Glancing quickly we hurry by
Guilty, while in our warm beds we lie

JESUS came for these, the lost
The sinners, the addict, the dealer
The hopeless, at all cost

HE fed the five thousand
Three, one day too
With just—one; on a street corner
—What will you do?

~

February, 2018
HUNGRY
{Prophetic}

For THE SPIRIT OF THE LORD would say
To the hungry, the thirsty, the down trod
I will raise up MY rod
A new day has dawned
The battle has worn on and on
Enemy of shame, I will end his reign
The enemy wounds,
Transgressions, bruised and broke
Who put powerful chains on you
I will choke
The pain taker, gain maker, usayer
FRIEND of the friendless
BREAD OF LIFE
I will be for you
If you will be MY wife.

~

February, 2018
TRUE HUMILITY

True humility I do seek
From those who

Claim to be at MY feet
Pour out your heart, begin to weep
Eternal judgement, you shall reap
Repentance flows for the unlovely friend
Clean *vessels* I seek
For this there is no end
Absurdities you claim
A harlot's reign, *a masquerade*
A facade, a fake tirade
Dipped in a thread of slippery grace
Usurped authority in its place
Dead men's bones tell no tales
Corpses rotting now in Hell
Before the gate of pearly white
You have stacked a sacrifice
Ear of corn, planted as fruit
Summer's proof will make me puke.

~

July 1, 2018
DINNERS READY!
{Prophetic}

Dinners ready, break open the wine!
Let's have good time!
What's that honey?
You feel funny?
You look fine.

Kind'a flutters in your tummy,
Woe!
Wait a minute, that's a no go.
A present you say?
Gon'na be a daddy someday?
Report for duty, gon'na be a cutie,
Reap what I sowed?
Eyes wide open now, I'm a no show!
She insists, got her wish.
Cream of the crop,
Gon'na your world rock;
Around him you'll flock.
Bastard child, this is getting wild...
Remember when,
I said, *"Abort that baby!"*
Oh LORD!
I must have been crazy!
Look at him now.
My wild child,
Grinning from ear to ear
—I live for him to rear.
Oh LORD, it don't get no better than this.
What great joy, what bliss.
Look at what I would have missed.
Oh world, I say to thee,
Don't close your eyes.
Don't turn from these.
Remember forever, and evermore,
These children are directly
From Heaven's door.

~

February 6, 2019
TRUE HUMILITY

Joy divine,
Children of mine,
Handed to you with a kind
Hand.
Acceptance you say?
Not okay!
About their face,
My love I sent your way,
In the face of your child
Today.

~

THE WORD THROUGH MOSES

I call Heaven and Earth to record this day against you,
[that] I have set before you
life and death, blessing and cursing:
THEREFORE CHOOSE LIFE,
that both thou and thy seed may live:
Deuteronomy 30:19 KJV

WEST

PUT IT BACK ATTACK
REPEAL,
REDEAL,
REVEAL.
NEW AND ANEW,
GOD'S TERRITORY FOR YOU
AMERICA, AMERICA
WASHED UPON YOUR SHORES
GREAT REVIVAL AS NEVER BEFORE.

~

February 12, 2018
WEST U.S.A.
{Prophetic}

Antagonize, don't despise!
Shake up, wake up,
A mountain is about to erupt.
Rumbling deep within the earth,
MY SPIRIT is about to birth
A plan from disaster.
Creative miracles is what I AM is after.
A diamond in the rough,
Believers get ready for greater stuff
Fresh anointing will flow,
When lava blows.
Hot rocks, molten sparks,
And showers of fire; breaking open hearts
When this begins,
Untold millions pouring in.

~

April 4, 2018
A POWDER KEG
{Prophetic}

A powder keg about to blow
Riveted

MENE, MENE, TEKEL, UPHARSIN

We will watch the show
History in the making
A shaking a quaking
Luxurious [1]spots
Transparent thoughts
Surely I will show
Super courage for to know.
Trembling Cabinet in the land
Knowing they are in my hand
A fistful of dollars
Squeezed from the skies
Resulting from mud in the eye.
A sinfulness exposed.
Credit goes to show
Lucifer again, he's no friend.
Triumphant changes, we will walk.
[2]Showing up they only block.

[1]*I believe this to be the Hawaiian volcano, 2018*
[2]*I believe the last half is referring to Oklahoma, teachers'*
walk out.

~

March 17, 2018
SURPRISE
{Prophetic}

Unbridled desire,
Unbranded waves

[1]Of raw power.
Inertia massive,
Overthrowing passive.
Glued to T. V. set
Overcome with sheer strength of size.
As it gets
Bigger by minute
Bursting its top.
Alive rock,
Hot molten lava will blot
Out the skies,
Revealing the size
Of gargantuan surprise.

[1]*Hawaiian Volcano Kilawau*

~

April 9, 2018
GROUND SHAKING
{Prophetic}

Ground shaking
News breaking
Headed to bed
Turned T. V. on instead
Electrifying, a show
Grow, grow, grow
Gargantuan in size
A supersonic massive surprise

A shock
Witnesses
A congregation gathered
Weather
Talk about size
Pray for this hour
A chance to escape
Brash decisions make
HOLY GHOST heard
Cancel
Red alert!!!

June 4 2018 Hawaiian volcano erupted. "Kilawau" literally means spewing out.

~

October 15, 2018
MISSION ACCOMPLISHED

Mission accomplished it seems
Caused many to dream

To the left and to the right
It shall go with powerful might

Stripped of all the right
It shall cause many to fight
Believers rally around the pole
Causing many to know
Bakers dozen twin oaks

Foolish dream many folks

Shamp agreed
For this book there is a need
President Trump will crow
Causing all to know.

Visions upon the world
Into Hell I will hurl
Casting spells and much more
Belong upon the evil's door
Return to sender to the lot
Build a wall with all you got
Grieve not THE MIGHTY SPIRIT OF GOD
Be real careful where you trod.

Haystacks and pumpkins on the door
Fit the Christians no more
Decorate for Halloween?
Know it's evil can be seen?

Children lined for candy
It all seems real handy
Be still before me
Children praying I have need
Wash your hands and hearts too
Causing many forward move.

~

September 17, 2018
ACTORS AND ACTRESSES

Actors and actress now in the news
They been given naughty reviews
THE KING OF GLORY ushers in
A new age for film now begins
No longer on the silver screen
Walking the streets
Unemployed it seems
Mocking THE KING
For all HE'S worth
They will bow
When HE hits this Earth

A hungering and thirsting now begins
For righteousness that never ends

Cosmotology reversed clientele
Rehearsed
Dense as fog that smog
Clean air, revered

Russian attack from the back
Peace treaty, real needy

Open doors slammed shut
Captives from us they thrust
Naval enable, code red

Ships afloat, standing down
No we won't, we will stand our ground
Patience, patience wins the race
Sheer delight as it takes place
Doctors and children all eyes to the skies
We're about to see—a giant surprise.

~

May 2, 2018

A CAULDRON BOILING HOT

In a cauldron boiling hot
Bring MY Church to the pot
There lukewarm you do sit
Oh, Church hear ME—I shall spit
Desperate are these children cries
Brazen rebellion you do despise
Calling on MY own
The hour is late—respond!
Rise strong MY people
Stop the wrong
Run, don't delay
Seek MY FACE
Pray, pray, pray
Oklahoma under attack
Don't turn back—seek ME!
You have heard

~

March, 2018
CALIFORNIA

There was gold in the west
When California was at it's best.
Land of milk and honey
Grapes galore and T.V. funnies
Golden shores kissed by Heaven's sun
Believers went there
A beautiful race to run.
Azusa street couldn't be beat
GOD'S favor for every flavor.
Deuteronomy 28:1-14
Every blessing you have seen
But, raging fires and mud slides galore
Don't you imagine MY WORD
You abhorred.
Demons dancing in the street,
Beating their chest as they repeat
Our god is ourselves
To thine own self be true
Where will you be when you are through?
Cast aside, left behind
Waiting for another sign
Run, I say for the door
Repent, get moving before
I close the ark

Just as in Noah's day
It's getting ready to depart.
Deuteronomy 28:15-68
Repent!
Don't be late!

~

May 12, 2018
OPENING A DIAPER
{Prophetic}

Opening a diaper
Fear and dread
Dirty your hands?
Abort instead?
But, wringing your hands,
When invaded you'll cry,
Why? Oh, JESUS—why?
Muslims, Isis,
Mexicans and more...
A whole lot invading your shores
Our shores swallowed up by typhoons
Our forests burned out when we need a monsoon
Fire ascending in lakes and streams
And a whole lot more like we've never seen

Look to your history,
Look to Israel's past.
Who kept the ancient ways

That did last.

When were [1]captivities
Given and turned?
When were children
Killed and burned?
Graven images on your shores
Idols, a stench on your doors
Children murdered
Their blood on my floor
Direct correlation ?
No?
You say?
America's not Israel,
We're Christians today

Look upon your golden shores
Blessed or cursed?
Need I say more?

Fire and famine, borders unsure.
Dancing in streets by *homosexuals* and *whores*;
School-children afraid, slaughtered today
Roaming violent gangs in the way
Another nation about to crash your shores
Preachers preaching peace and prosperity
When death of your own is all I see
Repent! Cry on your knees,
Return to ME!

Abolish the 'god' of [2]Molech!
Then MY blessing you'll see.

Deuteronomy 28 - Blessing or cursing?

[1]*Leviticus 20:1-5*
Those individuals who fail to head God's Law by condoning abortion will surely face God's Judgement if they remain impenitent. As noted in Leviticus those who sacrificed his child to Molech and those who closed their eyes to the sin faced the judgement of God.

[2]*If you want to know how abortion (the murder) of innocent little babies by the millions started? And what is behind it? Just look to the ancient pagan deities, i.e., Baal, Saturn, Molech, and Rephan. These blood-thirsty so called 'gods' have always demanded the horrific mass slaughter of children throughout history.*

But how does one start a study on these ancient pagan 'gods'? Just start digging into and studying about our modern 'holidays' and you will discover plenty!

~

May 2, 2018
CALIFORNIA CRIES

California cries
For your rulings
They despise
Open their eyes
"Jiminy Christmas"
They will all die!

Shuck your course,
Of a different horse!
Return to ME,
On bended knee.
Open THE BIBLE on the table,
Prepare your children's souls—you're able!

～

December 9, 2018
WASHINGTON STATE

Washington State
Before it's too late
Hear GOD'S song
Right the wrong

Killer whales you protect,
And yet, you snap little babies necks?

Liberalism is your way
Breathe of air does display
Your lack of respect
Fear THE LORD
Before...?
Oxygen rare!
Mask muss your hair?
Disheveled look?
Read THE BOOK!!!

Our FATHER WHO art in Heaven

THY will be done!
THY KINGDOM come!
On Earth as it is in Heaven.

~

February 15, 2018
ILLUMINATI
{Prophetic}

You think I don't see
I'M gon'na shine a light deep in thee.

Expose this sin and shame
You won't want this fame.

This country I'M gon'na shake, rattle and roll
Hold on to ME tight—here we go.
Love not thy sin, cast it away
Repent, begin again.
Out of the [1]ashes a newness shall rise
For ashes you will see, they will fill the skies.

[1]*Smoke and darkness blankets northwest Seattle, Washington and Portland, Oregon, once lauded as two of our cleanest cities in the nation, were being weighed in as two of the worst in air quality in the world. Fires along the west coast are causing smog, and breathing problems; for this cause, people wearing masks in the streets for breathing purposes are a common occurrence. According to a report in USA Today, Aug. 22, 2018 California is currently burn-*

ing: Carr, Malibu, Paradise and other towns ravished as ashes are filled the skies over Hollywood.

~

GOD BLESS THE WORLD

GOD bless the world,
The boy and girl;
Children everywhere.
JESUS had children gathered around HIS knees.
Pictures in THE BIBLE of these.
Stop them not from coming to ME.
What a verse we love to rehearse.

Of course they must be born,
If you please.
Before they can get to JESUS' knees.
Babies, babies, I hear their cries.
Oh JESUS, they didn't even bury us—WHY?

Narcissistic attitude
Washing their hands
With no gratitude.
Strangers to their own children's cries.
I blow Heaven open,
As I arise!

Feel the real heartbeat Bill,
No kill, it's real.
Jack and Jill went up the hill.

Try again
Tumbling down.
No amount of water from the skies,
As I hear these children's
Suffocating cries.
Split the dam wide open,
You'll see,
When you reverse this hedonistic atrocity.

~

April 7, 2018
COME AWAY

Come away, [1]come away
MY beloved
Come away, come away
MY Dear

Like a [2]roe walking in the meadows
I AM calling you; hear
Tenderly whispering MY NAME
It is very clear
An overcoming beautiful
SPIRIT OF JESUS
Is calling us near.

[1]*My beloved spake, and said unto me, Rise up, my love, my fair one, and come away. - (Sng 2:10)*

²My beloved is like a roe or a young hart... (Sng 2:9); cf. Sng 2:17; Ja 4:8

~

March, 2018
ONE MORE TIME

Muster one more time
All who are MINE
Get ready stay strong
Blowing over coals of ashes
Enlivens and makes whole
Fanning fires: flame blows
Sweep over my soul

~

CAST INTO THE LAKE OF FIRE

Cast into the Lake of Fire?
Flames licking higher and higher?

No!!!
These are gathered around ME.
They do sit upon MY knees.
With laughter and giggling of these
ME
They do please.

Justice
'I AM' is after
A god-awful sacrifice
Spilling blood of innocent like flies
Forgiveness???
Yes
Yet you will see.
I AM bound by MY WORD for these.
Hearken unto ME,
A fool only,
Ignores these pleas.

Laughter may ring around MY throne
But souls of these children are your own.

❧

March 17, 2018
ACRES OF DUST

Holidays in the fields,
Will [never] again yield.
Acres and acres
Of dust.
Clean water a must;
For I'm about to bust.

~

April 30, 2018
DREAMS
{Prophetic}

Bloodcurdling screams,
I hear in the night.

Crazy dreams about,
Wrong being right.

Children marching in the streets,
Warning parents don't be beat!

Pools of blood,
Mounds of bones
Belonging
To babies of our own.

History channel in the making
Text book revolt
Don't be taking

Children vain with imagination
Craving attention, feeling rejection
Like an ocean

Crazy are these dreams
Persecution of Christians
Also I have seen

Foreigners, storming our shores

Showing up in numbers
Never seen before

Mountains exploding
Oceans eroding
Standing in line
For food this time

About to wake from this unimaginable scene
I realize it's not a dream

~

KILL THE CHILD

Save the snow leopard,
Kill our child?
Preserve our environment, look forward,
Kill our child?
Dogs and cat's homes need repair,
Kill our child?
Protect the whales, they are rare,
Kill our child?
Illegal's children in a cage, you rage
Kill our child?
Be brave report child abuse or drug use,
But kill the child?
Terrible things, unseemly scenes,
Ruptured families and broken dreams
Yet, all the while

Kill the child?
Remember what GOD said
About innocent blood?
As we lay on our beds
And plead to HIM,
About the shape our country is in.
And all the while—
We are still killing the child..

∾

July 25, 2018
TWIN PEAKS

[1]Twin peaks,
Hot spot
Loose gravel,
Shot rock
Tons and tons of pepper spray
Visible fray

[1]*It is now October 2018. Protesters in streets of Oregon since confirmation of Supreme Court justice Kavenaugh. Fighting for rights to keep abortion. Cannons of pepper spray being used. This is happening in are where popular T.V. show *Twin Peaks was filmed.*

~

March 28, 2018
BELIEVERS GATHER

Believers gather,
Believers pray
Put away the food
Fast today
Grieve not THE SPIRIT OF GOD,
Decide quickly where you will trod.

Gluttony is a sin
Prepare yourself to obey
THE SPIRIT WIND
Delight yourself in MY WORD
Feed on it, you must purge
Turn to ME for a feast
Take control of the beast.

~

March 17 2018
WISDOM

Ask for wisdom
Kings and Queens have asked before
Answers to questions
They knock on MY door
Ashamed not to approach

Relieving apprehension
MY justice they awoke
Precious and valuable
MY time honored WORD
Pardoning sinners readjusting worlds
"Justice and mercy,"
I cry.
MY mercy runs deep as a river
Flowing underground in caverns to deliver
Precious is justice.
It goes hand in hand
For it,
I do demand.

~

April 29 2018
MORDECAI

Mordecai sat upon the gate
Telling Esther don't be late
She was born a Jew
Meant to rescue not a few
A Kingdom's Throne
She would sit
After the reigning Queen threw a fit
Removed, replaced
With shame's disgrace
A rise to power was Esther's hour

Untold millions would die
If she did not risk her life is why
Touch not mine anointed
Was GOD'S command
Reveille was blown
at the King's demand
A battle ensued that day
Because Esther was willing
And Mordecai fasted and prayed.

~

May 1, 2018
THE COMEBACK

Rocky Balboa appeared on the scene
Calm, cool, collected and mean
A cad, they shouted, an underdog
A joke whose broke
An underprivileged down and out bloke

But he trained unseen
Then put on the gloves and stepped in the ring
One punch, then two, ouch we're through.
No not I, when I wear a black eye
And blood down my nose.
I know where to go
Stretching my hands to the sky
I cry
JESUS my great deliverer

HE sets me up for a comeback
When life knocks you down
Your tough, you get back up
You step in the ring
And swing, swing, swing
Apparently devil you didn't hear me
When life knocks you down
I'll come back up with a rebound.

~

May 1, 2018
ESTHER PRAYED
{Written during Full Moon on Purim}

In the days of Purim of old
Esther was the Queen we are told.
She fasted and prayed and
The LORD obeyed
For her nation, it did save
A Queen?
HE did listen to a girl?
Oh yes, says GOD
For I gave her a scepter
A rod.
Lesson learned
Don't the rod spurn!!!

~

March 10, 2018
HOT SPOT

Holy ground I'm standing again
Festering spirit on the wind
Blow over my soul
Flame burn higher
Growing and leaping bounding desire
Beauty beyond control
Desire fired craving higher
JESUS only,
Brighter fire

Ashes grow cold, fire ebbs low
Darkness shooting in and a coldness begins
Just when you think that's all you got
A SPIRIT WIND blows in
And kicks up that fire a lot

Those coals are hot
Stir them a lot
Need I say more
I stand at the door
Forget not my children
I AM that hot spot

Hunger, come close
Thirst and be fed
Fuel for the fire

Comes from my coal bed

That fire however
Must be fed or
You will get nothing but
Ashes instead,

Hungering for more I stand at the door
I knock, open let me in
I'LL feast and dine with you again.

Rejoicing shall begin in that hour
Dancing around my campfire.

~

2 CHRONICLES 7:14 KJV
(CAPS added)

If MY people, which are called by MY NAME,
shall humble themselves, and pray,
and seek MY FACE,
and turn from their wicked ways;
then will I hear from HEAVEN,
and will forgive their sin, and will heal their land.

EAST

LEADERSHIP IN CRISIS

1 Therefore I exhort first of all that supplications, prayers, intercessions, [and] giving of thanks be made for all men,
2 for kings and all who are in authority, that we may lead a quiet and peaceable life in all godliness and reverence. – 1 Timothy 2:1-2 NKJV

We as believers are to pray for those in leadership and positions of authority. But just as the people have a responsibility to pray, so too, the leaders have a responsibility to lead correctly (lead the people in truth).

Sadly, in many governments world leaders are choosing sin rather than righteousness in their personal lives. Thus, their political motives are evil and their actions perverse. Unknowingly they have disqualified themselves from the very positions of honor God originally ordained for them.

Therefore, the masses have become mindless followers of lost men, who are ruled by the 'god' of this world, these are the 'spiritual wickedness in high places' Paul wrote about.

Jesus asked, *"Can the blind lead the blind? shall they not both fall into the ditch?" (See: Lk 6:39)*

In order to stop the current onslaught of evil The Church must take her true position of authority in Christ and begin to rule and reign on the earth. It is time to make every crooked path straight; as Ambassadors from

Heaven, we should be declaring HIS righteous to this lost world. Instead of subnitting to demon influenced [if not possessed] politicians, The Church should be the ones making public policy and laws.

We have no excuse? If our nation or any other nation is to ever line up with God's Word, it is up to The Church to bring it into manifestation.

~

November, 2016
SOON, SOON!
{Prophetic}

Soon, soon, soon
A new light will arise
Transparent as day

Hope for a nation
Covered in deceit
Cries of despair,
Lost in defeat

A breaking forth
A penurious light
A hope, a way
A cry of delight

GOD has called
A mighty man

A [1]Trumpet will sound
Throughout the land

Like never before
Anything we've seen
A rising again of the green

Going forth this hour
A shilling's delight
Awesome in power
Great with might

[1]*Wrote this about President Trump.*

~

February 12, 2018
EAST OVER AMERICA
{Prophetic}

Underhanded rousting it will cease
In the kingdom of the East
Pouring in the oil and wine
Prayer is prevailing in this cabinet of mine

George Bush began a push
To rollover Mexican Clover
An extended hand from Melania can
Open doors never seen before

Canada is gon'na obey
As royalty comes this way

A flood bringing new breath
Praising JESUS it will rest.
A purging, vomiting out
Many will scream and shout
Boiling up within the land
A President must plan, plan, plan
A gut's desire
Pushing higher

~

May 1, 2018

NEW SHERIFF
{Prophetic}

A new [1]sheriff in town arose
A lawmaker for the undertaker
Addressing the widow maker
From evidence unseen
Appearing on the scene
A rosy shame
On the cheek did appear
From this far and near
For we never knew
A heartbeat you could hear!!!

[1]*On a larger scale the President as head of the Executive Branch [acts much like a local Sheriff] ultimately seeing that justice is carried out for all, including the unborn. President Trump is this new Sheriff.*

~

March 15, 2018
A GEM
{Prophetic}

A [1]gem—*a diamond in the rough*
Brave, bold, gotta be tough.
Boiled in oil
Yet, I kept John alive.
Crazy redemption
I sent in the spies
A crimson cord of grace
On the wall did fall
Tattered and torn
Battered but borne!

[1]*I believe this describes President Trump. I believe he is that crimson cord of grace being extended to America [in this hour].*

~

Winter, 2017-2018
WAR POWERS
{Prophetic}

The Trump is lining war powers up
Pacifist cry, but he won't lie
Melania's boots won't root
She has power for this hour

Delighting herself in this reign
No mercy will she constrain.

～

May, 2018
GAME CHANGER

Game changer
Stranger
[1]*Lone Ranger*
Happy face sticker changer
Grave rearranger
Abortion changer

[1]*Pres. Trump has stood alone*

～

July 8, 2018
CHARGING UP THE HILL

I awoke at two in morning, I heard this as I awoke.

[1]***Regulations my ass!***
I wasn't asked.
Despair I declare
You climb out of that justice chair
Overcoming all
That [2]ruling will fall.

Self-pity you jerk, you won't work
Amongst all, you'll fall
The hardest.

[3]Trump run!
Show them I mean business
The HOLY GHOST smoke, will leave them choked
Let alone broke. Breathless, out of air
Remove him remove him, they will declare
Trump falters not, he won't stop
He's in the soup, but he won't stoop
Fear not [4]tiger's stop.
Unusual repair going on up there
A grace given

Heartache, mistake
Chapter and verse
Jezebel wake, wake!
[5]*Luciferian* reign,
Change, change
Opening Pandora's Box
Will this world rock
Wrest not, reporters flock
[6]Chalk talk.

Captain, captain I declare
A [7]bumpy road beyond despair
Smooth transition, reckon not
Animosity shock, shock!

[8]Charging up the Hill
Will thrill kill

Keeping up is tough
Keep going *Roeing, Roeing*
Register for fall
Important for all!
Bourgeois affair no more
Report time short,

[1]*The Lord is talking about the ruling of Roe Vs. Wade. He certainly wasn't asked about this before it was enacted.*
[2]*Roe vs. Wade*
[3]*God is moving thru our President. He is willing to hear The Spirit of The Lord and return the land to righteousness.*
[4]*Tiger stop is reference to his dealings with Asian countries.*
[5]*I believe reference to Catholic pedophiles and much more that has tried to take our country down.*
[6]*Chalk talk? Outline in chalk around dead bodies?*
[7]*A bumpy road transitioning our country.*
[8]*Capital Hill*

∾

October 20, 2018
DEUTERONOMY DAYS

On the march, on the march!
Hey, how about that starch?
As our President stands before an incredible scene;
Foreigners storming our shores, unbelievable!
What does this mean?
Deuteronomy days 28:34

Driven mad by the sight of them coming at our shores.
How does GOD this redeem?
Repentance for sure is a needed thing.

Top of the list: GOD does insist.

Children aborted?
Stopping of this reported

Days of Solomon? Pray for all of them
On *Capital Hill*; GOD given wisdom
Our destiny to fulfill
Stop abortion America! Lets rehearse,
Vote pro-life and reverse the curse!

∽

September 25, 2018
NEW THINGS TO SHOW

Captivating my soul got things to show you that will unfold
Not regular things but *visions and dreams*
Manifesting in the arena of Earth's scenes
Crime-infested cities revolt
As another regime takes a hold.
Foolish pride, laden with lies
Returns upon the head of the spies.
Glorious rise of barren things
Children's eyes behold their dreams.
Awakening the dead; Halloween we no longer dread
Witchcraft's fool, rebellion's tool

Cast into a molten pool.
Deuteronomy colossal as hidden [1]fossils
Behold the rise for foolish eyes.
October scenes just another means
As happenings unbelievable unfold
Drama falling as destiny is told
Troubled skies, a breath of cold blows
Redeemed from fire, children and animals goes
A docket a court
Time ends real abort:
Suitcases in the snow, nowhere else to go;
Clandestine retreat, books of many (millions) we meet
Golden opportunities all around we shall see
[2]Transparency in *Trump Towers* there shall be
Hit and miss books unfold director's meeting will be told
Magic stuff this is not.
A rise comes from [3]*Camelot.*

[1]*Many fossils are being discovered in Israel today, that are lining up with The Bible's historic account.*
[2]*News (real news) is being broadcast from Trump Towers.*
[3]*The White House*

~'

July 2, 2018
COVER YOUR REAR

The Left is screaming and fighting
It's because of Baal they are biting

Demons screaming for bloodlust
Torturing children is a must.

Enter Trump
MY deliverance:
Give MY children a chance
Let them go!
Same as HE told Pharaoh
What? Where? Not a chance!
Ruin my money making dance?
Bricks and mortar and stone
These children I own.

GOD said, I'LL say it again
Against ME you will not win
MY children killed
I know you know
Birth despair, another lair
I told Pharaoh fleas and lice
And blood sacrifice
Don't forget, I can be—not nice.

Panting and chanting and foolish ranting
Deliver me from Trump—I wanna be free
I'LL warn thee
These things have been brought about by MY power
I'M raising him up for this hour
"Give me the strength," he prays to ME;
"Please help me JESUS to be what I'm supposed to be."
You voted him in,
You cried for this man,

For I heard the Christians' prayer in the land.
Now, I'm gon'na do what I have said
You better get ready,
You better cover your head,
Things gon'na change around here.
Believe ME when I say—run!
[1]Cover your rear!

[1]*This was in response to the people marching naked against President Trump.*

~

August 14, 2018
HORDES OF HELL

The hordes of Hell
Pounding,
rushing Sounding
Fearful gigantic,
overwhelming
As they do swell
rising to overcome
The ONE GOD has appointed
for this very hour
Pharaoh's Army on his heels
Comprised of the enemy
Run by democratic wheels
Chariots resounding
Back against the sea

Children in hand
Screaming
"GOD ALMGHTY help Me"
"Where are the
Christians in the land?
Where are those for whom I stand?
Get in the fight?
Help me stand for what's right"
A red sea, is what I see
Rising from THE HAND OF GOD ALMIGHTY.
Enemies captured?
Nay, enemies swallowed
By the red wave.

~

March 7, 2018
CHESS PIECES
{Prophetic}

Chess pieces on a chess board
I AM moving this hour
King to pawn taking over power
Queen's knight I am moving
To the right
Jumping over some
Removing others
Capturing pawns
Proving lovers

To the left and to the right I shall go
[1]Rearranging the board, MY love to show.

Harbor not any sin, be not stubborn
You will not win.
With childlike faith, you should wait
Your turn will come, I'LL not be late
Remember
In MY game of Chess
MY *love always wins*
For I AM the best.

[1]*God is rearranging on the earth, much, many, and any are being changed. The Spirit of God is moving: people, things, positions and even places!*

~

July 1, 2018
ANCIENT OF DAYS

ANCIENT OF OLD,
ANCIENT OF DAYS, ANCIENT OF WAYS
Nothing new
What once was, shall be again.
Tower of Babel
Rebellion
You won't win.
Trying for a divide?
Leftist regime

You better hide.
Scooting under a rug
Holding your sin, hiding and hug.
Jeepers creepers
Filthy sneakers
Open shame should be your game
Repentance
On your face fall
Remember, HE is holy when you call
HE would that [1]none would perish
That to HIS SON JESUS all would cherish
But… *What once was, shall be [2]again*
If you continue
To relish your sin.

[1]*cf. 2 Pe 3:9*
[2]*cf. Ecc 1:9*

~

July 18, 2018

VATICAN'S REIGN

The Vatican's reign; upset reign
Tower came
Crashing down
Filling sound
Of noise heard round
[1]Found from precious tiny eyes
Little spies

[1]*We are currently watching this unfold as Catholic Church pedophiles are being exposed.*

~

April 28, 2018
GRAVE ROBBERS

Grave robbers
You will be
If you will report for MY duty

Secret society
Nah!
We will shout
Rout the enemy out
Desperation cries have risen
I despise
Demanding sacrifice
So you can look nice

Lay aside thy pretty clothes
Wear those that bring about birth

A fitting sacrifice for these
A battle on the knees

~

June 3, 2018
A DOG DIED

A dog died, a dog died
We all cry.
Look at what they have done.
Oh LORD how far we have come
An animal, no less
Such duress
Now let us address
[1]How dare the airlines treat us like this.
Revenge! Recompense!
Diatribe defense!
"How loud you shout
From MY inner courts without
I hear you pout
Devout
You make ME shake with rage!
Your sincerity over the death of an animal in a cage."

YOUR WORD oh LORD
Psalm 140:4 Protect me oh LORD from the wicked
who plot my downfall

A Great disastrous evil
Despising
Sick to the core
Arising

My tummy feels funny.
Oh, it's okay honey
Off to the doctor we go
It will help us.
An ultrasound shows
Life!
A heartthrob!
You sob?
You cry? My life you despise?
But
Let a dog die
And a nation will arise!

[1] *Wrote this after a dog died in baggage compartment of an airplane. Nation throwing fit about it.*

August 7, 2018—Dead baby found in plane toilet at La-Guardia Airport left by pregnant teen. Barely a ripple in the news over this. Nation not arising over death of our babies. However, I assure you The God of the Universe is.

∾

June 11, 2018
BENCH QUESTIONAIRE

A bench questionnaire
I rarely [1]declare.
Sits atop
Unencumbered
Retribution's number

Divine intervention repeals
More recompense
I [2]declare.

[1]*When the Lord gave me this I knew it was about my cousin's daughter, who is being falsely imprisoned for the crime she did not commit.*

[2]*It has been six years now. When I questioned The Lord as to why He was giving me this, I begin to understand. God is arising for innocent blood, although there was a conviction, there has been NO JUSTICE for that child. God will have Justice as His Word declares. Mercy also as this family has suffered much injustice. Since writing this I have witnessed a new bench questionnaire arising in the mishandling and injustice of this case. A new investigation will be forthcoming and true Justice served in this case.*

～

February, 2018
TIMIDITY RAGES

Timidity rages throughout
The land
People pushed back by
The devil's hand
Power for the hour
You shout and cry
Encouragement needed

For many do die
Hope has arisen
Showing up unimprisoned
Fetters unreigned
Of broken chains
Powerful presence
Of holy hope
Blessed redemption
Of love I stoke

~

April 24, 2018
MYSTERY
{Prophetic}

Financial gain shall come about.
Treasures hidden, you shall shout
A Peach Tree shaken in the wind
Protects all when knees do bend
Summer fruit, rotten heat
Cast about for all will eat
Summer changes
Rearranges
Certainty soon will be
Only standing close to ME

[1]Mystery
Obamanation
Could shape nation

Hear the rattle
Crisis pattern
More to come
Begun to run
Brace yourselves!!!

[1]*Drew wavy pattern on paper. didn't know what it was. Realized later it was like the patterns of a wave (or Richter Scale). I know God is not pleased with Obama changing His ordained Law of Marriage. Homosexual marriage law is an abomination to God.*

～

March 19, 2018
LOOK TO THE HEAVENLY
{Prophetic}

Look to the heavenlies [this hour]
Riches pouring out without power
Grace and mercy reflected
History in the making; inspected.

Blank sheets of racing power
Justice raging in this hour
Leave MY Trump alone
For I will protect MY own.
A rotten fruit I will remove
Prepare to exit on MY cue
Stay rooted to the spot?

It's OK;
For I will blot.
Tapering down feel ashamed
[1]Herculean effort to remain?
Power you say?
I'LL show you power.
A fearfulness shall leave you speechless
In that hour
Gripped by *a spirit of fear*
For I will draw near
On television they will say
Get him out of here
He must have gone mad

[1]*We are witnessing all this as people against Trump try to stay in office. God is removing the evil and corruption.*

∽

March 19, 2018
THE LAME BLAME GAME

The lame blame game
No win,
Great shame
Reporters beware!
I will begin to split hairs.
Jeans tangle and things jangle,
Wrapping up the news
Many will sing the blues.

Our President will win
For I have called him!

~

March 28, 2018
VICIOUS REPORTERS
***{Prophetic concerning Sarah Huckabee Sanders,
Trump's Press Sec.}***

Vicious are reporters
Crowding Sarah like a hoarder
Seeking vengeance for rebuke
Keep on going, GOD will puke
Fighting for her in this hour
She shall take a [1]higher bower.

Press; like a juicy piece of meat
You think you chew, ravage and eat
Moving closer breathing down your neck
A choicy bit I do detect.
Prepare your new report
For a heathen's retort
Face a giant in the [2]wind
See if you can against Him win!!!

[1]*When she was viciously attacked at the White House press
dinner. Sarah chose to maintain composure and take" the
high road" bringing much admiration to her throughout
the country.*

[2]*The MSM bias against Trump is to being exposed. No longer do we have factual reporting but opinions. These have reigned and become the norm in reporting. As God's Justice, i.e., "Giant in the wind" arises we will see the lies exposed.*

Press Secretary Sarah Huckabee Sanders has been listed as one of the 10 most admired women in the United States—God has surely vindicated her.

~

May 24, 2018
INNOCENT BABIES REPORT

Where's the news for these?
A disaster you declaring
A secretary, what she's wearing
Opulence fairing,
Bemoaning, bursting
A drop in the bucket thirsting.
A rock-hard place to be
When I come back you see!
Every eye will see and every knee
Will bend to ME!
JESUS will be there.
Angel armies do declare.
Racing MY WORD to say
But you
World news
Who choose

Tangled webs and jangled beds
Perverse reports, lax retorts
Chilling aborts of babies?

I despise your lies!

Normal news,
Lactose blues
A girl, a boy, a bundle of joy.
Crystal clear, a heartbeat I hear!
Chilling report, babies abort!

Instead you give
Left-minded struggle
Reporting muggled
Choppy blues
With short reviews, ugly news
Impeachment reviews?

Never real truth!

Cock and bull
You think—you fool!
The GOD of the universe!
Now I arise, for the motion
I despise.
Hammered truth
You shall see.
I will be in the midst of thee
Double trouble
There will be, If I don't see a reversal
Of this grave atrocity.

Grapes of wrath
Came at last
A breathing problem there shall be
Choking millions
We shall see
Just as these babies
Are choked before me
A staggering report
Oh News,
Where's your retort?
A [1]global rise of the ruling I despise
I hear these children's cries
Enemy's [2]lies I override

A doctor's report?
Let's not abort.
I just detected
A heartbeat.
Protected!!!
That's the news
A blessing's review
No abort
We now report!!!

[1]*The Obama Administration pushed for foreign aid too fund overseas family planning (abortion).*
The first act of our new Democrat-controlled House was to introduce a bill to fund worldwide abortions.
[2]*April 2009 – In an act of disrespect, Obama nominated three pro-abortion ambassadors to the Vatican; the pro-life Vatican rejected all three.*

~

October 5, 2018
BAAL'S RULING

Come on *Kavenaugh*
Baal's ruling will fall
Evil decisions? Foolish divisions?
[1]*GOD sits in the heavens*
Laughing in derision
At the rebellion of it all
No longer do they play
Getting meaner by the day
only one thing matters
[2]*Arise oh LORD*
And let your enemies be scattered

[1]*He that sitteth in the heavens shall laugh: the Lord shall have them in derision. - Psalm 2:4 KJV*

[2]*cf. Nu 10:35; Ps 68:1*

~

March 17, 2018
HILLARY—TIME WILL TELL
{Political Prophetic}

Hillary Clinton time will tell
Will see the inside of a jail cell

Obama'nation at his best
We're committed East to West
Colored lights will flutter out
Deactivate that color
They will shout
Rule against this mighty sin
Purification will begin
Putrid is the stench I shout
For I will take homosexuality out
Repent!
I say again,
For Lucifer will not win.

~

February 15, 2018
THE ASP AND ADDER

Gon'na shake, rattle and roll
Vibrations and reactions across the country
Calling for gun control
The View, a poison asp
Gon'na flee from the wrath.
Tongues a wag'gin', tails a fly'in'
On dignitaries they be lying.
Just as Jezebel in the streets,
Blood never ran cold
Before the [1]dogs licked it, we are told.
Harlot's shame, fortune's game.

No longer gon'na reign
As for the pure and simple rest will come
As for the evil, they will run.
Short and round, tall and thin
You gon'na see GOD begin to cull them.
Watch your mouth, control your tongue
Fly it not open, except to praise someone.

[1]*cf. 2 Kg 9:33, 35-36*

~

March 1, 2018
INSANE
{Political}

GOD gave me a vision
And people call me crazy I'm told
Visions are all through THE BIBLE
New Testament and Old

I have no claim of insane.
But you want your *"moment of fame"*
[1]Riding naked, body painted
In a cold north wind,
Or running streets with hats
Like [2]private parts on,
Does my mind bend.

You proclaim sanity
Yet you behave in profanity

Acting different than you proclaim
Makes me question,

Are you insane?

Joy Behar on The View
Questioned *Vice President Mike Pence* too
If you hear THE VOICE OF THE LORD
[3]You're a nut, you're abhorred

It behooves you to belittle
MY Vice President
With claims of needing mental resident?

Let ME assure all of you
Very, very, soon
You will hear A VOICE too!
A HOLY VISION will appear
As JESUS says, "look up here"
You will see
As you bow and bend your knee.

If I'm wrong what does it matter the cost
If your wrong, you will be lost.
[4]*E-v-e-r-y knee will bow.*
E-v-e-r-y tongue will confess
From the east to the west.
JESUS IS LORD

[1]*In Pennsylvania they hold the annual naked bike ride, with hunreds if not thousands of naked bodies pedaling through the streets.*

²*In 2017 we saw women take to the streets opposing the Trump administration doning hats and stocking caps fashioned in the shape of a woman's vagina, while still others dressed (or half dressed) completely naked from the waist down.*

³*February 13, 2018 "The View's" Joy Behar mocked Vice President Mike Pence saying him hearing the Voice of God was near 'mental illness.' She would later make a [very publicized] apology to calm the unsettled masses that objected to her attack on Pence.*

⁴*For it is written, As I live, saith the Lord, every knee shall bow to me, and every tongue shall confess to God. (Romans 14:11)*

~

March 15, 2018
LET MY PEOPLE GO!
{Prophetic}

Joy Behar
Sat up in bed and said,
"Who is this man called JESUS?
Who messes with my head?
A VOICE, I do hear," says Joy Behar.
Crimson stains on HIS hand
Nail scars was the plan?
Scared to death, *"I shall attest*
The truth I see

Made public for me!
For now, I will bend my knee!"

~

August 31, 2018
MUTINY AND TREASON

Mutiny and treason
Of MY beloved without reason
Account I must give
For what has been given
Earned not by a living
Original form, paradise's trust
But now? A question thrust?
Turning away from the things that we know
Giving ourselves over to a sideshow
Believers know I appointed the man
A higher power only in JESUS stands
Stood tall and very strong
Did only good, no wrong
Brewing a nasty cup
Witches spilling lies erupt
Tending the fires of Hell
Coffee in hand, stories do tell
Get another retort
Let's find another report
Believers I cry to thee
Find shame in watching these lies I see

Allied troops need stand at your doors
Enemies about to climb your shores
Rally, rally, rally I cry
Trump by MY HAND I gave to you is why
[1]Forfeit not your deliverer today
[2]Look at the fruit of what he does do; I say

[1]*As in the days of Samson the children of Israel did not recognize the deliverer the lord had sent but tried to tie him and hand him over to their enemies. (See: Jdg 15:10-14)*

Wake up Church! Back Trump!
[2]*Recognize what God is doing in our nation.*

~

June 20, 2018
A CAUSELESS CURSE

Wrote this after Peter Fonda's malicious attack on Barron Trump

A causeless curse shall not alight
Black is black, and white is white
Devoid of sanity
Curses of humanity
Be careful what you say

Children caused to be put in a cage?
Be fearful of THE LORD
These are HIS anointed you abhor.

MY looks with perceptivity

Repent quickly of thy depravity

To Mr. Fonda and all
Who continue to curse *GOD'S* anointed

It is a fearful thing to fall into the hands of a living God.
- Hebrews 10:31
AMEN!

Hollywood Actors elitist seem to think they have the right because of their wealth to take a political platform and stand against our President. God's Word says in (De 8:18) It is God who giveth thee power to get wealth. To abuse your power and wealth to stand against the man God has anointed is a very scary thing. God says: touch not mine anointed. (cf. Ps 20:6, 105:15; 1 Chr 16:22) Hollywood and any others should take heed.

~

June 20, 2018
TO FIRST LADY MELANIA TRUMP

Be still
Don't be stumped
No way will I allow this to overcome your [1]child
Appointed, anointed,
to ME she cried
"Oh, GOD me they despise
But not my son
For what evil has he done?"

GOD says:
"Arise stand strong
It won't be long
I will vindicate you
Before it is over an apology too!"

[1]*I also heard this one after Peter Fonda tweeted ugly threats against our presidents son Baron. Mr. Fonda did in fact later apologize for this.*

~

YOU FILTH, YOU TRASH
{President Trump}

You filth, you trash
You gnaw, you gnash!
You despise the rise
Of the man of power
I have appointed for this hour?
Is he not the [1]tool in MY hand,
Given a plan to restore the land
To righteousness?
For pollution, I have a solution.
Again I say,
Evil for good you return.
Watch MY people
You shall learn.

[1]*cf. Pr 21:1*

~

December, 2018

INNOCENT BLOOD ON OUR HANDS

This country cannot stand
With *innocent blood* on our hands
True to form every known norm
It is now a divided forum.
Greatness will either rise or fall
When CHRIST'S enemies come to call.
Apparent now in the scheme of things
Fruit of the political machine
Winds of change blow across the earth
Bringing famine, floods, earthquake, and dearth.
And yet in the good ole' USA,
Cries for blessings crash in waves
Separation from Church and State
Gives the enemy a mighty gate
Template of the scheme of things
Brings only brighter scenes
Hunger and thirst for righteousness
In JESUS put your trust
Blessed are these basic foundations
But overrun with evil temptations
Get your hands off of us!
According to the ones who trust
In 'the god' of *Molech* and *Baal*
They would see this country fail.

~

May 1, 2018
TO TRUMP
{Prophetic}

To Trump it shall go, go, go
Blood of innocent
Reversal Roe, Roe, Roe
A giant wave shall sweep the land
Gives way to a cry of another brand
Giant stories in THE BIBLE
Praying for their survival
A special needs session
Breaking open prayer in the land
Food for thought
Plan, plan, plan
Church rises up and begins this move
Hoping to prove
Innocent blood
Reversed for love.

~

September 22, 2018
LEANING TO THE LEFT
{Prophetic}

Leaning to the Left might seem alright

Til we remember what started the fight.

Bloodcurdling screams, as necks are snapped
Forgiveness? Oh please—our prayers are lax.

Angrily, live and let live
As children to homosexuality we give.

Concentrating on [1]myself
I put religion on a shelf

Fornication and lil' porn,
About these did JESUS 'really warn'?

Investigative writing is really cool.
When it's not used as the enemy's tool!

When my numbers up, it'll be ok,
JESUS, I know and *I'll fly away.*

Weather reports were forgiven of sorts
Relishing sin, we wouldn't let JESUS in.

Helpless cries float about
As in *socialism* we do doubt!

The crash of 29 on our mind
Money making consumes our time

Signs of the time. Peer pressure, we mime.
Allowing our thoughts to be ordered like robots.

Preachers preaching on the radio
What's that? Oh, something from long ago.

No longer having a holy fear

Wisdom no longer they hear.

Man has forgotten once again
JESUS remind us
YOU'RE THE SAVIOR from our sin

We need JESUS that's no doubt
As we humans in sin flounder about!

[1]*cf. Ja 1:27*

~

PROVERBS 29:2 KJV
{Written by the wisest and richest king that ever lived, King Solomon of Israel}

When the righteous are in authority,
the people rejoice:
but when the wicked beareth rule,
the people mourn.

ABORTION

Are you young, unwed, scared, or alone?
No where and no way, to give this baby a home?
Cry out to JESUS, HE will show you the way
It's not HIS desire for this baby to die today.
Cry out to JESUS, and then call on the phone
'Adopt-A-Baby' we'll find this precious child a home.

National Adoption Hotline
1-800-923-6622

[1]*Jesus told him, "I am the way, the truth, and the life. No one can come to the Father except through me." - John 14:6 NLT*

[2]*God is our refuge and strength, always ready to help in times of trouble. - Psalm 46:1 NLT*

~

April 23, 2018
A VOICE FOR THE VOICELESS

A *Voice* for the Voiceless,
YOU *called* me to be.
A Voice for the Voiceless,
They're dying daily.

~

AWFUL AND DIFFERENT

Awful and different,
I do warn.
About innocent blood
Of the unborn.

The following excerpt is from [pgs 45-46] of **"Lace, Lust, and LIES** — *Our shameful affair with the Porn Industry"* by Aaron Jones.

SCENE OF THE CRIME

Everyone knows The Bible forbids both fornication (sex outside or before marriage) and adultery (sex with some one other than your spouse). Few people know that in many states and towns, laws are still on the books that make it illegal to have sex with anyone other than your spouse. So then, two people having 'casual sex' are actually commiting a crime (<u>sin</u>) against themselves, God, the laws of the land, and society.

> *1 Corinthians 6:18 NLT*
> *Run from sexual sin! No other sin so clearly affects the body as this one does. For sexual immorality is a sin against your own body.*

> *Hebrews 13:4 NKJV*
> *Marriage is honorable among all, and the bed undefiled; but fornicators and adulterers God will judge.*

DEAD BABIES TELL NO TALES

According to the Urban Dictionary a 'cleaner' gets rid of evidence like bodies, blood, weapons, fingerprints, and <u>even witnesses in order to hide the proof</u> or notion of the crime.

God showed me that is <u>a perfect description of abortion.</u> Two people commit a sexual crime (sin) and then guilt, shame and condemnation demand they have the only witness killed (removed). Since Roe vs. Wade there have been over **62,000,000—MILLION <u>tiny witnesses</u>** 'cleansed' from our sexual crime scenes. THINK ABOUT THAT!!! Their body, blood, DNA, inherited characteristics—the proof; ALL stripped from the scene before they ever have a chance to point to Momma and Daddy.

THE HIGH COST OF TOMORROW

If this is our harvest so far, try to imagine the horrifying harvest we have coming if we continue down this path of sowing to every fleshly whim and desire!

Luke 13:5
I tell you, Nay: but, except ye repent, ye shall all likewise perish.

Payday is coming! ...and I'm afraid the price for all the evil deeds which have overtaken us will be far too high.

∾

February 12, 2018
TIME TO REVERSE

Time to reverse
Roe vs. Wade
Abortion on demand
Gon'na exit the stage

Abortion's an issue we don't like
Much as it's painful
[I speak from experience in my own life.]

Survival of the fittest
In the species; we say.
However give them

Survival in the womb as they lay.

Everyone I sent to Earth
Was sent by MY SPIRIT
With a [1]*purpose* to birth.
A [2]missionary, a statesmen, a banker, a lawyer
A mother, son, husband, father, brother, sister
or daughter;
A soldier, a teacher, a president or two ...?
Tens of millions more before we're through ...?

A great reprehensible,
Reprobative,
Holocaust
Lies at your door.
Blood of your children
Dripping at MY FEET
On the [3]floor

I'VE Watched as they [4]cried unto ME
[5]Screaming in horrible pain and misery.
This insanity breaches the cloak of MY grace!

Disposable humans...???
[6]They lie in your land waste.

Ripped from the womb
Tiny brains shattered
Limbs torn asunder
Their lives did not matter!

[7]MY EYE is upon the whole human race.
[8]This is way beyond a national disgrace.

Untold millions carry MY cross

They *lift holy hands*
Then cry I'm at a loss
Tell me, oh LORD. What do I do?
Show me, oh LORD, I'll work for YOU.
Abandon the sin of convenience, I cry
Wash yourself in *the blood* I provide
Pick up *the sword.*
Carry your *cross.*
Soldiers are willing,
No matter the cost.

Begin to telephone a friend
Call your statesmen
Tell them
It's time to put an end
To Abortion on demand!
Gather together begin to pray
Let a wave sweep this nation
Begin it today!
Sons and daughters
I'M calling thee.
—Repent!—
For 'the god' of Molech
Must bow his knee!!!

"Wake up Church!"
I say to thee
"Time for millions to march with ME.
Abortion must cease throughout the land

This I lay on you with a heavy hand!"

Untold millions more will die
If you don't wake up to their cries.
Lift up your voice
Repent out loud
Shout to your congressman and senators.
Do it proud!!!
Let your voice be heard with one accord.
— "No more abortion!"—
Saith THE LORD.

No matter the cost,
I went to the cross,
I died for your sin,
Thank GOD
Mary let ME in!!!

List and letters unbreak fetters

■ Sign petition today go to: *www.themoraloutcry.com* ■

End Abortion!

[1]*Before I formed you in the womb I knew you. Before you were born I set you apart, I appointed you as a prophet to the nations. (Jeremiah 1:5)*

[2]*But when He who had set me apart before I was born, and who called me by His grace. (Galatians 1:15)*

[3]*Thus says the Lord "Heaven is my throne and the earth is the footstool of my feet. (Isaiah 66:1)*
Heaven is my throne and the earth is the footstool of my

feet. (Acts 7:49)

⁴And He said "What has thou done, the voice of thy brother's blood is crying out to me from the ground." (Genesis 4:10)

⁵They sacrificed their sons and daughters unto devils and shed innocent blood. (Psalm 106:37-38)

⁶You slaughtered my children and offered them up to idols. (Ezekiel 16:21)

⁷The eyes of the Lord are in every place, keeping watch on the evil and the good. (Proverbs 15:3)

⁸These six things the Lord hates, yes seven are an abomination to him; a proud look, a lying tongue, hands that shed innocent blood... (Proverbs 6:17)

~

April 14, 2018
BLAST OF HIS NOSTRILS
{Prophetic word against Roe vs. Wade}

With a blast of HIS nostrils
¹HE breathed into man.
With a blast of HIS nostrils
²HE parted the sea and made dry land.

³Fear HIM, HE says
⁴Fear THE GREAT I AM.
Fear ME today,
I AM marching through the land.

MY EYE is on the [5]sparrow;
I see them fall.
Does MY [6]EYE not see,
What you call
—A not at all?

Babies, babies
I hear [7]their cries.
—Aborted—
—Gone—
In MY FACE they rise!

Cries from these children
Have risen aloud.
Cries from [8]these children
Would make Hitler proud.

Breaking apart
[9]MY grieved heart.
Open *the windows of Heaven*, you say?
I'LL open you 60 million empty graves!

[10]Odious,
Rotting corpses of babies.
[11]Justice, I AM is after.

Playing 'church'
Won't get you the prize
[12]Bearing burdens
Attending the cries,
Bringing reversal
For the ruling [13]I despise.

Brace yourself,
Bend your knee,
Cry unto ME!
Go before THE THRONE,
—[14]Repent—
For the sin of your own!

[1]*And the Lord God formed Man..and breathed into his nostrils. The breath of life. (Genesis 2:7)*

[2]*With a blast of THY nostrils the waters were gathered together. (Exodus 15:8)*

[3]*The fear of the LORD is the beginning of wisdom. (Proverbs 9:10)*

[4]*Put them in fear oh LORD that the nations may know themselves to be but men. (Psalm 9:20)*

[5]*Are not two sparrows sold for a penny ...not a one shall fall to the ground without your Father. (Matthew 10:29-31)*

[6]*Thine eyes did see my substance ...when as yet there were none of them. (Psalm 139:13-16)*

[7]*For He who avenges blood unjustly shed does not forget the cry of the afflicted and abused. (Psalm 9:12)*

[8]*They band themselves against the righteous. And condemn the innocent to death. (Psalm 94:21)*

[9]*Even tho your mother forgets the child of her womb I will never forget you. I have engraved you in the palms of my hand. (Isaiah 49:15-16)*

[10]*Odious: − revolting, repulsive, repellant, repugnant, disgusting, monstrous, abominable, detestable, hateful,*

dreadful, contemptible, deplorable, despicable, atrocious, unspeakable.

[11]The Lord is famous for this: His Justice will punish the wicked. (Psalm 9:16)

[12]Bear ye one another Burdens and so fulfill the Law of Christ. (Galatians 6:2)

[13]There are six things The Lord hates, seven that are detestable to HIM, Haughty eyes, A Lying Tongue, Hands that shed innocent blood/ (Proverbs 6:16-19)

[14]If MY people who are called by MY name will humble themselves and pray and seek MY Face and TURN from their wicked ways, THEN I will hear from heaven, and I will forgive their sin and I will heal their land. (2 Chronicles 7:14)

~

March 17, 2018
ARISING

I had a vision, I saw GOD Himself sitting out in the universe on a throne. It is a big throne. As each and every baby was aborted and its spirit returned to GOD, He arose off His throne and caught each and every child as they arrived. He would then turn to his right and take them somewhere out in the universe. He has a special place prepared for them. It was a majestic and trembling sight to see Him arise. America and the world must understand God is arising for these children that are being aborted.

AGAHST!
I AM forced to tell
Little babies bound for Hell
Oh no, nay I cry
For in MY hand
I now arise
—Innocent blood!
That is MY cry,
Each child I greet as MY own.
Torn limb from limb.

[It's as if GOD was Speechless—there was silence]

Precious are these to ME.
Paganism is this
From MY so called
"Christian country?"
If you insist.
A festering,
Shaking AM I
MY blood boils at each cry.
From you, laughter?
It gags ME. ...I cry, I spit!
There lukewarm MY Church sits.

[I feel the disgust in this statement.]

You remember MY WORD:
To hate, what I hate;
To love, what I love.
To befriend the friendless,
To cry aloud—for innocent blood!!!

~

April 1, 2018
RESCUE THE PRISONER

Roe vs. Wade
Rescue the prisoner
Unbreak the chain
Gather together again
Repeal *the Abortion Law.*
Cry against it.
Let the gavel fall!
Trifle not with MY law of innocent blood.
Trampled on and shoved under a rug.
Running to the end of grace,
Crying for mercy I stand
In the place
Homosexual reversal
And abortion will fall.
Pick up your pencil
Hear MY call!

~

May 11, 2018
SURELY I RISE

Babies, babies
Surely

I rise
Below
I see
You despise.
Children
MINE
For [1]inheritance
Are thine!
Before you give them back to ME.
Murdered! Butchered!
A reward to ME?
Kindness of MY HAND?
Children in the land.
Be still and know for this
I'M going to show a reward to thee.
Paganism short
Reward, abort?
Fools despise?
Now I arise!

[1]*Lo, children are an heritage of The Lord; and the fruit of the womb is His reward. - Psalm 127:3 KJV*

∾

April 22, 2018
ELEGANT DEFENSE

Elegant [1]defense?
Justice sits on a fence.

Ferocious move of MY power
Gaining offense by the hour
Roe will go
Bold as a lion
Vicious, no whim.
Bringing justice
Will your knee bend?
Every knee!
Every eye!
Boldness for MY battle cry!

[1]*cf. Ps 94:20-22 KJV*

~

March 28, 2018
LIFE HAS BEGUN

Life has begun in a different way
Time to reverse Roe vs. Wade
Anchored tight, it's not a show.
Buckled up, here we go.
List and letters,
Unbreak fetters.
Abortion tools will not rule,
I will make them look like fools.
How dare this sin begin [1]again!
A bucket list you dare miss?
Choose life!
Declare right!

Stand long, stay strong.
V for—Victory
At the—Y.
Open legs!
Allow children's cries!

[1]*This is not a new sin, but one of the most ancient and detested sins. The sacrificing of our children is an evil abomination to The Lord. The OT false 'god' of Molech required children for sacrifice. We today sacrifice our children in abortion to the god of convenience. Every time this sin rises again in history, God warns us of the consequences.}*

They served their idols which were a snare unto them. Yea they sacrificed their sons and their daughters unto devils. And shed innocent blood, even the blood of their sons and their daughters whom they sacrificed unto the idols. (Psalm 106:36-38 KJV)

(See also: 2 Kgs 21:16, 23:10)

~

April 11, 2018
COMES TUMBLING DOWN

Roe vs. Wade
Comes tumbling down
City by city, town by town
Plunder the enemy

Take the stronghold
Rip from his bosom
Little tiny souls
Shatter the elements of his lies
Jumpstart the engine, open the eyes!
Hugging a tree you'll declare,
Purpose in your heart, don't harm the air,
Don't kill a bird, bee, or bear
They have a 'right to be'
What about that baby in thee?
What crime did he or she commit?
Inert being?
Thats all that sits?
What about you?
Who decided for thee?
About your birth?
A parent here on Earth?
Your right to exist was given to thee
What about this baby?
GOD says
Woe, woe, woe!
If you don't let MY children go!!!
I'LL stretch forth MY hand
I'LL darken the skies
I'LL do more than drown you
For I hear little babies cries!!!
Mercy I cry
But justice you'll see
By MY actions I speak
If you don't listen to ME.

[1]Listen to MY VOICE; hearken to ME
Reverse this repugnant
Belshazzar
Atrocity!

[1]*What does the Lord require of thee do justice and show mercy and walk humbly before thy God. (Mi 6:8)*

~

May 30, 2018
OCEANS OF EMOTIONS

Oceans of emotions
As I go Roeing
Returning to the scene of the crime
Individuals it will remind.
Old scars buried in a well
It was no accident,
Do tell!
Remember each one
Personal, as they clung
To a belief.
Now [1]they need relief.
[2]Forgiveness
—*Good News*—
GOD does [3]choose.
HE [4]forgives
When our sins we relive
Pouring out each heart

Bringing a ⁵brand new start!

¹*Abortion not only kills the innocent child, <u>it scars us on the inside.</u> Many woman have suffered inside for years with unhealed scars and old memories. Sin is sin no matter the action.*

²*If we confess our sins, he is faithful and just to forgive us our sins, and to cleanse us from all unrighteousness. (1 John 1:9 KJV)*

³*Keep in mind God in His great foreknowledge knew you were going to abort that child, commit that sin, etc. yet HE CHOSE to send His Son, Jesus to die for you anyway. God is NOT in the punishing business—He is in the forgiveness and restoration business; that is the heart of The Father.*

...But where sin abounded, grace did much more abound: (Romans 5:20b KJV)

⁴*If we trust in Jesus and ask forgiveness for our sins, just as His Word says, He is faithful and just to forgive and heal us of our sins and wounds.*

⁵*There is no sin that is too great to be forgiven and this includes abortion. Jesus' mercy washes and cleanses us when we turn to Him. He then sets us on the road to complete restoration and recovery—made whole; brand new!*

~

April 17, 2018
CAPTIVATING THE SOUL

Captivate the soul
Captivate the soul
A hungering, a thirsting
A joining together
A linking of hearts
Unbreak fetters
Embarrassment never
A coming [1]together

[1]The Word says to confess your sins one to another and to pray for each other that we may be healed. As we do this, it breaks the bonds and chains around us, sets the captive free and joins the body of Christ together. (cf. Ja 5:16)

~

December 16, 2018
SUFFER NOT

Bloodcurdling screams
Hellish scenes
JESUS redeems
Babies
Ghoulish dreams
Pitiful cries

Rise
As I
Waste time.
Cherish the thought
Their bodies rot
Land waste we fill
Delivered the kill
Blood money bought
Quartered, diced, and dissected
Inhuman neglected
Rejected!
Planted?
Beastly.
No marker erected.
Abandoned.
Standing before MY THRONE
In a room of their own.
MY children
Unique
[1]Suffer not the children
To come unto ME!
Great suffering is all I see.
A [2]millstone around my neck?
Better for me than one child I harm and yet,
Americans harming millions I send
When will this insanity end?
[3]*Watchman on the wall*
Hear MY call
Soon—trouble!
Diapers you say, to big a price to pay?

Children to messy? sacrifice Jimmy and Bessy?
I guarantee
Great sacrifice you will see.
Hearken unto me.
Abortion
You will flee.

[1]*cf. Mk 10:14; Lk 18:16*

[2]*cf. Mt 18:6; Mk 9:42; Lk 17:2*

[3]*cf. Is 21:6; Ezk 3:17, 33:6*

~

June 30, 2018
HOW DARE

Swinging in their daddy's arms
Safe from all harm
Beautiful,
A baby girl or boy
"Keep me as the apple of their eye"
Muster the cry
Below
All as should be?
Wait
Stop
Blow reveille
Great harm
Murder to these

Alarm,
Travel it takes
Wake MY Church, wake!
Business as usual
No, no, no!
Church get ready
Time to go
Hardship for some
Oh GOD! Help these little ones
Traveling the land
Time to expand
Orphans these be
Fatherless are these
Shortly I come and I will see
Those who have visited these for ME
James 1:27

Cry to the body
Scream out loud—stop!
The killing of the child
Innocent blood
Red river flood
The lust of Baal
Reversed
Rehearsed
Cry for you will thirst
Forgiveness
For those who have omitted ME
Repent on your knees
While you are still able

Darkness is falling
Push back from the table
Declare a fast today
Obey, sacrifice?
Oh MY Church
These cries are of the butchered
Twice: Once in the womb
Then again, as they leave the room.
Collagen prepared
For your *face cream* there

How dare!!!

~

October 1, 2018
PRAYER WARRIOR

Babylonian times you pine?
With the *enemy at the gate*
Watchman on the tower,
You cower and hide
Reward inside?
Nay I say
MY Bride shall shine in this hour
Radiant replete with power
Overcoming all the enemy will fall
Turn the cheek, mild and meek?
Yes, I say
But not when it comes time to pray!

Prayer warrior, servant Bride
Kingdom shaker
The enemy has nowhere to hide
Brave as a lion. Ferocious and bold
Devouring enemy territory she never quits or lets go.
This is the sound that is music to MY ears
What is this noise I hear?
MY lover, MY Bride
As she draws near!

~

April 28, 2018
ISLE OF PATMOS

John on *the Isle of Patmos*
Saw fit to obey GOD
Rather than man most.
He saw, then wrote a vision clear
That is still causing man to fear
Because of his obedience
Men know reverential expedience.
Revealing Heaven and Hell
Rejoicing brings birth of sinners to tell.
Short,
Sweet and to the point,
Spirit from soul
Every cartilage and joints.
Raptured Church do tell.

Redeemed
Being rescued from Hell.

~

CHILDREN

Children, children, children
That's all I hear
Children, children, children
Crying in GOD'S ear
My GOD, my GOD I don't want to die
My GOD, my GOD
Help me they cry
Tortured!
It's not enough,
Innocent blood you spill.
You gotta be tough.
Do you want to know
What I know?
Do you want to see
What I see?
Do you want to hear
The innocent cry of these babies to ME?
Reveille!
Report!
For I'M gon'na show
The beginning of the end
For your mind to blow

Each step I'M gon'na capture,
Choicy, delect they are after
Tender flesh
Precious eyes
Little children's bones
They despise
Strange enough how little are these
Sold for valuable property.
A sickening thing has been uncovered
Swept under a rug for another lover
Money—the love of, the root of evil
Worming its way
In their heart like a weevil
These lives a breach of brevity.
Hopelessly *murdered* in depravity.
Belonging only to Satan
No more for his murder
I'm hating.
Proverbs 6:16-19

∾

September 29, 2018
RU-486

Here's *the money trail*
Straight from the pit of Hell
Grossly understated
Advertisement R-rated

Now in pill form
Abortion from big Pharm
Christine Blasey Ford
Her lies we now record
Cheap sacrifice?
Oh, America you better think twice
'RU-486' —The pill that kills
America, America, we are in a fix
This will be our downfall
if this drug we don't recall
Abortion at will, from Capitol Hill
Reverse the kill

~

May 20, 2018
THUNDER

Thunder I hear
Life is short
GOD stomps
No abort
Collagen sits atop your face cream
Such a thing, I never ¹dreamed
Darkened tragic represent
Horrid offering I present
Sacrifice?
You don't think twice.
Rocked by official report

Creams keep selling
No abort?
No outrage?
No front page?
Heaven raises it's brow
With justice arising now
Creams selling, I despise
For youthful appearing eyes
Where is your tears?
Pushed aside for fears?
Of a wrinkle on your brow?
Actually I hear now
Enough

[1]cf. Jeremiah 19:5

～

DANCING ON THE DEVIL'S GRAVE

Dancing on the devil's grave
Shopping carts, empty raves
Obedience sacrifice
Telling all they don't look nice
Honey your money
Brings nice new things
But I heard the screams
It took to buy your [1]face creams
Shook foundations of the world
Proving time around you does not hurl

Buying, stocking all you got
Will not relieve the shock
Horror and pain
For all your worldly gain
Of the cringing stain
That does remain
Of the putrid shame
Of one baby's pain
For your
Moment of fame!
Reject those face creams and cosmetic tools of the liar
Return I say to a higher power
Dreams of collagen down the drain
Open saving of children
No pain!!!
No gain!!!

[1]*Much known fact, collagen from aborted babies is in many of American skin care and cosmetic products. Yet we continue to buy!!!*

～

SILENT THE MASSES REMAIN

Silent the masses remain
As I expose the pain, sin, shame, and stain
Of an industry, filled, with the horrors that be.
Asleep at the wheel.
MY Church

What will it take?
A jerk, a knock, a cry!
The fields are white
Cry I
No longer wait
What does it take?
A shake and bake
Awake!

~

September 11, 2018
GOD PLAYS HARDBALL

GOD plays hardball
Justice is screaming out,
Demanding a brand new game plan
Rules have now changed, *all bets are off.*
GOD is now scrambling the [1]board of all cost.
Heavenly teams are beginning to form,
Casting aside even known [2]norm.
Welcoming committees crowding the aisles,
Boldly stand, wildly cheering
As GOD brings out 'the child'
A team? A choir? A host!
Millions upon millions, stand unopposed,
Opening the roles of those who have walked the throes.
Butchered
Aborted,

Travesty,
Justice lost
Heralded now by
GOD
CAPTAIN OF THE HOST
They are of MY making, MY ³team, GOD does boast;
Opening the game with *a coin toss,*
GOD glares at Satan, *"You lost!"*
Then HE calls, *"Play ball!"*
As mighty hurricanes begin to fall.
Calling to man *"Look out below"*
As gigantic winds begin to blow.
Hunkered down in derision,
Man still scoffs,
Foolishly continues in his division.
Even the angels do wonder
As GOD now stomps through HIS thunder,
"Batter up, swing"
He pitches the ball
Fast low and hard
It plows through Earth's yard.
One, in the lesser Antilles,
Two thru Hawaii as I please,
Three, that East Coast I'LL ⁴rock the most.

Cries now began to arise, prayers float about,
As people do wonder, *"Help us,"* they shout.
"MY *actions speak louder than words,*
even MY enemies this have heard."
"Repent of thy abortive ways."

"Watch out!"
Now come some giant waves.

Movie goers spellbound?
Something from the giant screen it sounds!
Nay I say
It's just GOD having HIS way.

Relentlessly they have challenged
Opposing GOD'S delicate balance
Of justice and mercy for all.
Now through weather it comes to call.
—60 million plus—
I wonder...?
Those who should be so meek and mild
Are now MY team of aborted child.
"Touch not the apple of MY EYE"
"For I still hear the aborted's cry"

When I wrote this [strangely enough] on 9/11, the weather map of our Northern Hemisphere showed nine different hurricanes on the [1]board at the same time. Even weathermen noted it was a very odd, sci-fi type occurrence, and definitely not the [2]known norm.

Satellite views of these [3]nine storms (like a team on a field) looked suspiciously like hard balls (curves, fast balls, sinkers, sliders, etc.) being pitched simultaneously at the land.

At the time of this book's release, [4]hurricane Beryl passed through the Lesser Antilles, then Hector and Lane in Hawaii; also, hurricane Florence on the East Coast.

~

May 3, 2018

VIETNAM CHILDREN

Vietnam children were killed,
and then they were burnt.
This was real.
A burnt fact, an offering of war.
Bloody enough.
But no more.
Retribution for them has come
That was one war we never won.
Deemed a necessity,
Termed an atrocity.
Victims of war!
Now addressing children
More victims of war.
Only this time
More than before.
Medical atrocity?
Convenience, necessity?
Children offered on *the sacrifice of Baal*
Termed a necessity, trying to send them to Hell.
Each and every one
I gather as they come,
To the aborted babies
[1]I rise.
Children, MY children

They sacrifice.
Heaven's retribution!

It won't be nice.
A close encounter of a divine kind?
Reality Check—
These children are MINE.
—Murder—the charge,
Victims of war no more.
Grieved, horrified; I cry
Muster MY army
MY chosen ones; I cry
Sweep in a wave
A new road paved.
Close the grave.

Unmitigated circumstance?
With love I'LL reverse this happenstance.
Choices reverse
Chapter and verse.
Innocent blood,
Redeemed through love!

~

EVEN THE HORSES
SCREAM GOD'S NAME

Even the horses scream GOD'S NAME
Declaring the heavens open

Proclaim
Justify
[1]Winner Triple Crown
How come?
Why?
Dare I decry
Justice
Will open the skies
As I arise

[1]*God has spoken thru and about horses all through history. 'Justify' winning the Triple was a sure signature of God arising.*

~

April 2, 2018
A JEALOUS GOD

A jealous GOD is
I AM;
Promoting fear of another brand.
Great mercies have I shown.
But now I AM calling on MY own,
To keep their promise made to ME
To bow and bend their knee.
Repentance power,
Comes from prayer
This hour!

~

April 29, 2018

MY DADDY'S BLOOD

My daddy's blood
Cries from the ground
Spilt when no one was around,
Murdered?
No, ...suicide?
—maybe?
But just think about little innocent babies.
Shunned, unprotected,
Aborted
—Murdered—
Broken, and naked.
Blocking a memory, I must arise
For my own child's blood
I hear the cry.
Beautiful little boy or girl (*Adam to me*).
Oh baby, I'm so sorry
Forgive me please.
Empty arms I raise
I hope and pray GOD'S mercy each day.
Dry my eyes,
Arise,
Battle gear on,
Report for duty;
Run soldier run!

~

April 29, 2018
A WOMAN'S CHOICE

A woman's choice?
Wait!
You spew hate, murder, abomination
Use babies for bait?
Fools blathering and cruel,
About abortion
—You won't rule!

Choices you make?
About face,
Run liberals, run!
Acronym [at paradise's gate (pg)]
They gather daily.
A fool's choice; dance rejoice?
Cradle your head at night,
Console yourself (you done right.)

—*ISIS* has more mercy than this—
Their cruel religion at least on birth insist.
—Blood of innocent?
They don't care?
You cry help me?
They arc invading here?

I'LL give you a choice,
Simple and free:

Avoid destruction,
Bow your knee.
Shame, shame, shame for your lies.
Your children are homeless,
And I hear their cries.

Rivers of blood of these
Pool at MY feet.
Mercy for innocent
Will you march for these?

Don your [1]*birthing hats* back on
For I saw when you marched and shouted in fun.
Beast, beast
Be still before ME
A tear in MY eye?
I'LL crash your party!
I'LL do more than cry!

Foolish remembrance of these?
I'LL give you remembrance
A party if you please.
Rivers of blood will run
I'LL darken the skies.
A birthing, you despise
A commencement you'll see
For I'M about to cry—mercy.
But justice you'll see!

Her flowing tresses; I'LL fly.
Blood of the innocent, is why—

MENE MENE TEKEL [2]U

[1]*I wrote this after protestors marched in the streets of Portland, Oregon against President Trump's administration and to keep their right to abortion. These protestors wore (donned) hats fashioned to look like a woman's private parts.*

[2]*I saw a hand extended (I think it was my own) about to write UPHARSIN on the wall... but the Holy Spirit stopped me at the 'U'. Why? Because, this is where we are in the prophetic timeline (endtimes). [It's done! The judgement has been rendered.]*

∼

April 28, 2018
FROM THE AFRICAN JUNGLES

From the [1]African Jungles
Year of the unborn
Believers will gather,
For them I warn.
Working a great work I see
Abortion, you will bow your knee.
No fancy name will I give to thee,
For murder is plain and simple to ME.
A gasping cry, a desperate lie
Born of sin to deceive again.
Lucifer you won't win!

Flowing tresses under MY flag march

Battle cries, a victory arch.
Stand and hear MY alert
For these children I'll send
[2]Justice to the earth.

[1]*36 percent abortion rate among African American woman*
[2]*What does the Lord require of thee but to do justice to love kindness and to walk humbly with thy God. (Micah 6:8)*

When justice is done it brings joy to the righteous, but terror to the evildoer. (Pr 21:15)

[2]*Let justice roll on like a river, righteousness like a never failing stream. (Am 5:24)*

$\sim$

April 17, 2018
EXECUTIONER'S CELL

Children in an executioner's cell
Waiting for judgement.
Being condemned.
Bound for Hell?
Wait a minute,
A trial, I did not get.
A jury? A judgement?
What crime did I commit?
Lonely, oh so lonely
My cries,
"Help [1]me JESUS!"

They rise to the skies.
"GOD I need you please
Stop this sin!
I did nothing!
Why?
Am I being condemned?"
Hold your peace my child
For only a little while.
For I will condemn
Not on a whim!

—Justice—

Raises her flowing [1]tresses
Brazen murder of children
She does address this.
Overflowing
She arises
Retribution for the
Murder of innocent
She despises.

[1]*The Spirit of the Lord is upon me. He hath anointed me to preach good tidings unto the meek: he hath sent me to bind up the brokenhearted, to proclaim liberty to the captives, and the opening of the prison to them that are bound. (Isaiah 61:1 KJV)*

~

BLIND MAN

A blind man shall see
Abortion shall be
The death of us all;
If we don't repeal the call.

~

July 20, 2018
ABORTION DOCKET

Let's show Hitler
What we mean,
When we show up
On this scene.

Abortion docket
We will rock it
Alive arrived
Do tell...
Reprieved from Hell

A child, I cry!
Nay, no,
Not I
But THE JUDGE of all
It seems
Will scream
A just and holy GOD
I AM
Remember that
When life is in your hand!

Am I not [1]THE JUDGE of all flesh?

[1]*cf. Ps 9:8*

❧

December 11, 2018
PIVOTAL

Born again!
Christian!
That's what I am
And yet to Hell
I'm willing to send
Unborn babies
Little children
Unopened eyes
Tiny toes
Moving cries

Reckon not
They are not real
—Pivotal—
Unwilling to kill?
Living in darkness
Just don't seem real
Let's not talk about it
Voting to kill
Push that button
Despise
Once more
Blood of the innocent
I don't hear their cries!

~

August 26, 2018
RISE UP CHURCH

Rise up Church!
March for life,
Put an end to murder and strife.
Strife is deadly, it ends in death.
—Abortion is murder—
Let's put it to rest.
Put the enemy under our feet,
Cry to THE LORD; begin to weep.
Tears from Heaven flowing from THE THRONE,
GOD is weeping, these children—to HIM belong.

—Righteous indignation—
For now HE has arose.
Final judgement?
Are we in the throes?
Belittled? Beleaguered?
MY army I call,
Millions
Move
March in MY halls.
Take back this country,
Give it not away!
Open your hearts,
Hear what I say.
Choose you this day whom you will serve.
Deuteronomy 28
Blessing or cursing?

∽

October 4, 2018
ROSES ARE RED
{In Response to Planned Parenthood's threats to congressman}

Aborted you say?
You want your way,
And threaten those who say, nay?

Bruised, battered, beaten, and torn,
Ripped from the wombs,
Their limbs shorn.

Aghast! I declare,
You dare
Threaten the ones
That run the boat—
That won't float.
As rats on a sinking ship;
Beginning to understand their party
Is amiss.
Defiance in the face of A HOLY GOD
Planned Parenthood
Be real careful where you trod.
Rebellion and murder
On Capitol Hill?
Be careful I warn again
For you are standing against
GOD'S will!

Roses are red,
Violets are blue.
The LORD GOD ALMIGHTY'S
Got your number too.

～

June 30, 2018
WHY?

African jungles?
Sacrifice?
Cannibalism?

We don't think twice,
Not nice!
A husband we have,
Nice shoes on our feet.
Houses to live in pretty clothes, good food to eat.
Exceptional things.
Liberty rings.
Joy it seems.
Breath of air.
No despair?
Why
Are you committing
Sacrifice to 'the god' of *Baal*?
I won't be nice!
First law in *'tablet of stone'*
No 'god' before ME;
Rule of MY OWN.
Remember the children of Israel
Rose to play
When on the mountain
They deemed too long
Moses had stayed?
Remember?
I do!

Now you dare resurrect
This idol of Baal.
A cheap brazen sacrifice so you can look nice.

Gird up thy loins oh woman and man
Before ME I demand you stand.

Where are the children I handed to thee?
A gift from ME to thee.
Shuddering, I shake with rage
From MY FINGERS I hammer this page!
Oh people wake up and see
Reverse this hedonistic atrocity.
For a jealous GOD is
I AM
We have broken HIS laws
HE rules in this land.
We are made for HIM
Not HIM for us.
That's how it stands.

Belshazzar saw *the handwriting on the wall.*
Daniel warned him, *'You will fall.'*
America
Wake up!!!
We are a hair's breadth from that same trembling cup.

∾

August 26, 2018
BRUISED AND BATTERED

Bruised and battered
Beaten and worn
These are MY children
With these scars they have borne
Trials and tribulations, a heavy load?

Why don't you try a walk down their road?
Touchy subject?
Oh well, not today!
Blood sacrifices and you just set there and say, hey!
As sacrifices to hedonistic 'gods' you serve.
You think I look away and MY HEAD just swerve?
Think again MY Church;
Your waiting for the rapture and all the while.
I'M waiting for you the enemy to capture.
Deuteronomy 30:19—choose life!
That you and your children may live.

~

May 26, 2018
GOD'S RULE

To he or she who performs abortions.

Your gon'na learn this rule.
The GOD of the universe
Doth hate your cruel tool!
Hippocratic Oath?
You [1]fool!
That's your rule
Do no harm!
Have you forgotten school?
Aren't children harmed by your abortion rule?
Harmed!
Murdered I say!

And as a physician you receive your pay.
Mercenary hired to kill.
Slaughtered!
For this you think I stand still
I'M standing there.
Let ME make it real.
A heartbeat detected?
Thirsty for blood, that, you rejected.
[2]*Eye for an eye, tooth for a tooth*
That's MY rule.
To the grave and beyond
I'M gon'na show every fool.
I'M gon'na *upset your apple cart.*
I'M gon'na make it understood,
It better start!
You better close up shop
Looking down the barrel of
A twelve-gauge [3]gun,
Is gon'na make more sense
And gon'na be more fun,
Than the consequences of what I'M gon'na do
When you stand behind closed doors of
Just ME and You!!!

[1]*A Fool hath said in his heart there is no God.*

[2]*(cf. Exodus 21:24)*

[3]*This is an allegory and in no way is intended as a threat to anyone from the author, publisher or anyone on this earth. This however is God's Word about the unrepentant sinner on Earth. Abortion is murder, murder is sin, plain*

and simple. Even our laws of Earth reflect this. There are consequences for defying God's laws and without repentance and forgiveness which comes through the cross and the blood of Jesus Christ, we all will give account for our actions. I shudder to think of the consequences of standing before a holy God and having the murder of many innocent babies on my hands.

~

September 3, 2018
DRACULEAN

—Draculean Times—
Bloodsucking, raging rhymes.
Hitchcock could do no better,
For he never imagined these chains that did fetter.
Ghoulish tales and fairy spells
Claws of evil, wolves bedeviled.
Eyes blood red, peering instead
Seeking a hand grasping to stand.
Clothed all in white,
A deceiving angel of light.
Musky the smell, from the barrels of Hell.
As he does fill, his quota to kill,
Mastermind of delaying time.
An evil plot to terminate the lot.
Try as he might
He'll not stop THE TRUE LIGHT.

For I'VE issued a call
An Army!
We must stop them all.
What is this evil?
An ancient creature
Murder, he does feature.
What fills this bill?
Abortion
If you will!

~

November 25, 2018
HIDEOUS

Hideous evil, grotesque retrieval
Of a plan formed
To butcher the partial born.
Grasping life, gasping air
Abortionist parting hair.
Beacon of children born
Harm, of their brains now torn.
Retrieval of their skull,
Brains sucked by Baal.
A picture I form of the unborn.
Believe me when I say,
GOD doesn't want it that way!
America oh choose
To repent, for I say you have dues.

Due to the unborn;
Of the innocent blood you have worn.
A tide of red lies on your shores.
Evil is knocking at your doors;
Covered in the red.
I will send it back on your head!

Retrieval upheaval.

~

April 6, 2018
ENOUGH IS ENOUGH!
{Prophetic}

Enough is enough!
Time to wake up!
Time to get tough
Prayer I call
To one and all!
Crashing Hell's gate,
I'M about to create
Religion speaks of ME
Powerful prayer bends the knee
Religion runs its course: prayer warriors
Stay MY course:
Believers registered across the nation,
Forging war vehicles for an occupation!
Believers calling upon ME
Seeing a reversal of abortion to free

Lives ransomed from Hell's lust.
Chance opened for
Abortionless.

~

August 20, 2018
SOWING AND REAPING

Sowing and reaping is a law
Galatians 6:7 says it all
Whatsoever a man sows, he shall reap
This is GOD's law; it will keep

GOD [1]hates *the shedding of innocent blood*
But we as Americans for this, seem to have a love
The Earth is groaning for the seed we are sowing
The blood of innocent [2]cries to GOD above.

They are perishing daily
Hardly a thought given, as they kill the baby.
As The Church
How does that affect thee?
60 million plus have perished since 1973

*John 8:32 Then you will know the truth
and the truth will set you free.*

How about these babies entombed in a womb,
Awaiting the butcher's room?
There I declare, MY Church sits

It don't fit,
Not my sin!
[I Saw GOD cup HIS EAR]
Say again?
³*To know to do good and doeth it not is sin!*
Free? The truth shall set you free!

What about these babies?

Register to vote today
With *Roe vs. Wade* we must do away!

¹*cf. Pr 6:7*
²*cf. Ge 4:10*
³*cf. Ja 4:17*

⁓

December 15, 2018
BETHLEHEM

Hugging a tree
Hang some more ornaments, please
Christmas time in the air
Children expectant everywhere
Wait!
What do I see?
A whole generation down on their knees
Worshiping together
A star is born
To Bethlehem it rest that morn.

Giving peace to the world
A brand-new baby
A boy, not a girl
PRINCE OF PEACE
Righteousness
KING OF KINGS
Fruition?
From a babe in the hay?
The SON OF MAN and OF GOD
HE has a destiny to trod.
Fulfillment came
Simply because HE lay in the hay.
Mary, she was a key
For fulfillment of HIS [1]destiny.
Sacrificial her body
Life laid down for the child
How?
By giving birth, ain't that wild!
Milk of human kindness,
Compassion at play
Marvel ye not!
What [2]if it were today?

[1]*Every baby has a purpose for being born on the earth, every child a God-given destiny to fulfill.*

[2]*Abortion must be stopped.*

~

December 4, 2018
THE BLIND LADY

GOD'S laws are immutable and irrefutable,
Whether we like it or not.
They are in motion and they cannot be stopped.
Just as what goes up, must come down
The law of gravity
Will surely cause a fall to hit the ground.
What else is around?
'*The law of sowing and reaping*' does abound.
Goodness you sow, goodness you'll see.
Just as the corn sown shall the corn sheave.
The law of mercy and justice exist
Scales with the blind lady
We must never resist.
Handed the power of right versus wrong
Evil resisted must be our song.
When those scales have been tipped
Justice does right the rift.
Abounding also a little-known cried law,
We in America have allowed to fall.
The law of innocent blood;
It brings justice with a mighty flood.
Kings, and Queens, and President
Have ignored this, bringing the earth to vent.
Remember THE SCRIPTURE

Love what I love
And cry aloud for innocent blood?
Rebellion of the earth
Caused by rejection of the birth.
Children
Blessedness of GOD'S HAND.
Mass slaughtering in the land
Bringing about the
Justice
To fall on man!!!

~

December, 2018
A CLARION CALL

Blow the trumpet in Zion, Zion
Sound the alarm in *MY holy mountain*
Tremble you inhabitants of the land
Fear THE LORD don't you yet understand

Your children's blood dripping
From *the blind Lady's* hand
I will once again restore justice in the land
Blow the trumpet
A clarion call
Announce to all
Justice will fall!

~

ISRAEL STANDS

Israel stands still
As the horn does shrill
For remembrance of *the holocaust*
And the six million lost.
America, America
What *value* will ye place
On the cost of the sixty-million of thy children lost.
Justice arises
Abortion GOD despises.

~

REFORMED

Now you have heard the things I have warned
Now you have heard the screams I have borne
Abandon
Reject
Reform
About face
This ruling I scorn
Justice
Is MY answer.

What does the Lord require of thee (you), to do justice, love kindness, and to walk humbly with your God. (Micah 6:8)

NORTH

Psalm 82 TPT
The Passion Translation (CAPS added)

TRUE JUSTICE

All rise! For GOD now comes to judge
As HE convenes Heaven's courtroom!
Judges every judge and rules over every ruler!
Saying *"How long will you judges refuse to listen*
To the voice of true justice
And continue to corrupt what is right
By judging in favor of the wrong?"
"Defend the defenseless,
The fatherless and the forgotten,
The disenfranchised and the destitute.
Your duty is to deliver the poor and the powerless;
Liberate them from the grasp of the wicked.
But you continue in your darkness and ignorance
While the foundations of society are shaken to the core!
Didn't I commission you as judges, saying
You are all like 'gods,' since you judge on MY behalf.
You are all like sons of THE MOST HIGH,
MY representatives.
Nevertheless, in death you are nothing but mere men!
You will be laid in the ground like any prince
And you will die."
All rise! For GOD now takes HIS place
JUDGE OF ALL the earth!
Don't you know that everything
And everyone belongs to HIM?
The nations will be sifted in HIS HANDS!

~

February 12, 2018
NORTH
{Prophetic U.S.A.}

North
More and more
Forgiving near the door
With the trumpet din
A shout does begin
Rolling thunder, breaking under
Barriers without crashing about
A Sergeant's drill
Becoming real
Practice forgot
Blowing apart rock
Rushing in MY SPIRIT WIND
Fresh from disaster
Souls I AM is after
Explosion after explosion
North, running down
Fire consuming ground
Brace yourself, I say
Believers should pray, pray, pray
Concussions on the wind
Bravery untold about to [1]begin

[1]*We have yet to see this happen and pray it never does.*

~

HEAVENLY COURT

I make a motion to ascend the rights of the children
Heard in the courts of Heaven
Justice has arisen
Wisdom once fallen
Now comes calling
Earth and Heaven it appears
Now line up with heavenly cheers
Under duress the witnesses decline to confess
No crime have I committed, they declare
As they climb into the justice chair
Sorting facts by the numbers
The court renders—it thunders
A child innocent, blood has been shed—60 million
Requiring justice, to raise it's head
Action needed to requite
Motion approved with all our might
With a mighty trumpet blast
The courts of justice have convened at last
Heaven's Throne rights the wrong
Before long, restitution
Instated from a resolution
A fact Jack
Were about to reverberate from that!!!

cf. Joe 2:1; Jdg 9:23-24 (See also: Author's Preface)

~

June 22, 2018
EARTH MOVE
{To the tune of old song}

I felt the earth move under my feet
Under my feet, under my feet.
Crashing about in my head
A new tune GOD has said
Be anxious for nothing. HE has seen
For I AM that living stream
Drink of wells from MY supply
Ye shall live and never die!

~

May 22, 2018
FEMA

Fema
Shall overflow
People won't know where to go
Powered by a higher realm
JESUS' Church
Welcomes them
Come on Church I say to thee
Get ready
For very soon you shall be

The light to run to
I will shine thru thee.
To the left to the right
Not by power or might
But by MY SPIRIT
It shall be
For I will call MY army.
Heads up!
Look alive
For I AM arised
March MY army
Stay in step
Were gon'na
Wring the enemy's neck.
Be bold stay tuned
MY SPIRIT'S gon'na fill the room.
I'LL give a shout and you shall run
Be ready MY brave ones

{corrections}

~

May 1, 2018
SOUPS ON

Soup's on
Kitchen calling
Homeless
Boiling, tripping, falling

Catch the fever
Relief?
Bring her
Oh, MY Bride
Don't hide inside.
Obey MY WORD
Justice, you have heard!

~

September 29, 2018
SHAKE, RATTLE AND ROLL

The earth begins to rumble, shake, rattle, and roll
The dirt begins to crumble—here we go!
Church be prepared, we ain't going nowhere.
A battering weapon; a cry,
A holy body to arise.
Feeding the hungry, praying for the poor
An *at ease* Church no more.

~

March 17, 2018
GET READY TO RUN
{Prophetic}

Get ready to run
Horses are coming

Fathers moving
Some are leaving
Shaking awake, the hour is late
Removing all, changes wait
My hunger is about to burst
Salt get ready
Make them thirst,

~

March 7, 2018

NO HARM SHALL I DO
{Prophetic}

No harm shall I do, to those who come
No harm shall I do. Get ready to run
Darkened skies, lots of cries
Without power, a moving this hour
Families come pouring in
Famished for MY SPIRIT WIND
Broken pieces of their lives
You will see as I supply
Don't capitalize
Don your helmets, keep armour on
For the battle has barely begun
Hopeless, helpless thousands about
Glue yourself to ME, for I shall shout
Move MY army, begin to run
Boldness overtaking MY brave ones.

∼

February - March, 2018
BRAVERY SHALL ARISE

A bravery shall arise
A brand new boldness not disguised.
Lover's leap, it shall be deep.
Micro religions, they shall end
A cry for holiness it now begins.
How beautiful on the mountains are your feet?
Will they carry you
MY job to complete?
Compliance on you does rest
For they are coming from the
North, South, East and West.
A single drop of blood.
Is all they seek.
I shall drench them; they shall weep.
Covered in MY love
Wrestle not with flesh and blood.

∼

April 21, 2018
WHOLESALE RELIGION

Wholesale religion does not agree with
THE SPIRIT OF GOD.

It flounders under *the weight of truth*,
Counts not *the cost*;
Reforms not the lost.
Efficiently replaces power
With nectar of a self-seeking flower.

Shackles and bars,
Crosses and stars,
Far outweighs who we are.
Raging power, bluetooth tower
Wisdom comes from THE ONE
WHO sent HIS SON.
Now I see says the blind owl to me
Go for gold—sold out be.

~

April 24, 2018

ABORTION INDOCTRINATION

Abortion indoctrination I hate
Rebellion starts at 9 or 8
Seeking to repair the breach
A lost generation we must reach
Fitly jointed all together
A generation wants a father, a mother
Children seek their own devises
Doctors treat lonely empty crisis
Serious seeking of MY FACE
Is the only repair of the human race

Look not to the East, South, or West
But be prepared to the North
McDonalds this is not
'Having it your way' misses the spot

Catholic religion reality?
Tainted yoke, can't be broke?
Gobble, gobble; choke, choke?
Time for them to bend real knee
Crystal clear, choices see
Juicy tidbits
President Trump will expose these
Scandalous the President?
Wait till this they get a hint!
Arch-Bishop of a Diocese?
Prepare for all to hit their knees
Elections? Race?
Candidates some replace
Lucky you, when this begins
Changes from MY SPIRIT.

～

August 14, 2018
RESCUE MISSION

A Rescue Mission I'LL perform
Just watch
For this JESUS was born
Stagnation—be gone!

Mercy not worn
Great happenings, fearful cries
Over and under I'LL send MY supplies
Over and over you shall see
MY love flood the rise
Of a tidal wave as these cries
Rise to the skies.

~

July 8, 2018
AFTERSHOCK

Aftershock,
What a rock
Heaven and Earth
To church, Church
They will grope, no hope
Light shine, all MINE
River run, public display
Peter proved he knew the way.

Credibility on the Pharm?
[1]National harm joke broke
Hope has arisen, very soon
Childish dreams fill the room.

Humpty Dumpty on the wall
A cracked egg will fall
Genius and Kings

Will hang themselves it seems
Weighty rafters, heavy matters

Denver high, *Rocky Mountain* skies
Roe vs. Wade exit the stage
Rage, rage, turn the page

[2]College rejection Presidential Election
Stomping around, Casper found
College degree, relieve, relieve.

Staggering, you [3]choke
Grave decisions, I hope
Believers everyone
Bandwagon, run, run.

Animalistic behavior, you [4]savor
Globalist defeat, repeat, repeat
Capitilistic punch, crunch, crunch

[5]To *Boeing* you applied
Cried, cried
Work release

[1]*I believe this is Marijuana Ruling, and that unless there is repentance God is going to turn the pharmaceutical industry on its ear.*

[2]*Melissa Howard running for Florida State House caught in lie about her college degree. God is neither Democratic or Republican. HE is holy and righteous and is cleaning-up our Government. Truth is being required and lies exposed.*

[3]*California choking on fires. The grave decisions are the ones*

to reverse Roe vs. Wade. Calling ALL who carry the name of Christian to get on God's Bandwagon for pro-life. Register and vote this fall.

[4]Referring to Pedophilia being upheld by far left wing Globalist will eventually be defeated. Crunching the numbers President Trump is reversing our economy to prosperity again

[5]Could this be a future military buildup? Also, President Trump pushes for decent jobs for ex-cons.

~

March 19, 2018
A SHIP GOES DOWN
{Prophetic}

Slipping into a watery abyss
A [1]ship goes down
Its grave missed
Gliding upon the waters
Treading ocean
[2]Sons and daughters
Lowering boats as they race
Helicopters raising more up
Help is racing to erupt
On the waters they will float
Praying, praying for a boat
Surely I will send them in
Guided by MY HAND they will win

[1]*Our faith is likened to a ship in the Gospels.*

[2]*As pornography and sex scandals are being exposed and abuse of the innocent revealed people wander floating on the waters of todays world not knowing which way to go. God is sending in the help to rescue these, Calling on the true church to be salt and light as needed. Giving guidance and restoration of faith in the One Who is Truth. Not looking to man but to Jesus our great deliverer.*

~

October 18, 2018

IRELAND

{Prophetic Warning to the nation of Ireland}

Mystical chapters of Ireland's coast
Wayfaring strangers they do boast
Retired chapters of *many kings*
Olden dances of maiden's dreams
Irish jigs conjure up
A cheerful gleaning of joy's cup
Bright and bitter has thy history shouted
Many wars have you clouted
For better days have you yearned
Return us not for our youth to burn
Bitter death you have seen
Brighter days you have dreamed
Now a turning upwards bound
Peaceful days it seems around

Given rest from GOD above
Decision
To return HIS HAND of love?
A matter grievous on your shores
Abortion
Of your children
Will again *open death's doors.*
Depart! GOD says from this decision
Ichabod you will see in HIS derision.
Blood running from thy womb's cup
Enough!
MY Ireland
It's again about to get rough!

~

April 29, 2018
SPOON-FED RELIGION

Spoon-fed religion
Hoovers above CHRIST SPIRIT
Shoved under a rug
Open you mouth, shove it in
Yum, yum, when will I win
Mixed with odious stench
Be brave, for I shall wrench
The spoon away.
We are done
Your not gon'na play

Christians calling on MY NAME
Being part of the game
Fool's paradise
You better think twice
I sent MY SON
For you to save
Water not THE WORD
Repent!
Obey!

~

March 12, 2018
A YIELDED VESSEL
{Prophetic}

A yielded vessel is the best
No glory will I share
North, South, East, or West

Eat at the same table
Cowboy coming, deemed him able.
Operating in grace
Bucking horses won't win the race,

[1]A shocking discovery rocking the world

Brothers and sisters bow their head
Lukewarm will I spit out instead

April shocking times

Marriages wholly I will forge

Days of hayfields, clover, and honeybees are over.
Roads repaired in the dark
Ashes falling it will start
THE SPIRIT OF THE LORD will say
For MY children a way I will create

A burning gulf we shall see
Waters afire it will be

[1]*I believe the Ark of the Covenant will be found and all the facts about its discovery will be made very public.*

~

March 28, 2018
ABORTION ODIUM

Easter time
You will know, know, know
Time for Wade vs Roe to
Go, go, go!
Waiting for it to begin,
This decision comes to an end.
Millions died from the whim.
Babies protect till the end.
Raising JESUS to the podium
We shall overtake an [1]odium

[1]*Odium - A general and widespread hatred towards someone as a result of their action.*

~

April 7, 2018
GASPING FOR AIR
{Prophetic on Abortion}

Not yet gasping for air
Waiting for birth
Little children—murdered by dearth
Year of death? Date began?
Not even a gravestone?
For these little ones
Powerful legislation shall arise
Proving of life for these little eyes
Defining legislature on the horizon
Giving way to new life arising
Justice shall prove
When life's conception began
A birthing shall move
To when life really ran
Hebrew 7:10

~

March 17, 2018
BRAINWASHED GENERATION

Time to go
Roe, Roe, Roe

Time to raid
Wade, Wade, Wade.
Hold not onto these words
Show the world
A boy, a girl
A tiny precious planted seed.
Repentance need
A sin begins to unfurl
Into Hell's pit I will hurl
—Abortions will end—
Brainwashed generation,
Offends ME!
All will see.

~

April 14, 2018
HE IS THE POTTER

HE is THE POTTER
We are the clay
And if we don't reverse
Roe vs. Wade
We will see that HE doesn't play
I made you and not you ME
You're gon'na understand
I'M not asking pretty please
From a viewpoint of your knees
I will shake and rake
And you will fall and quake

~

A TRUMPET BLAST

A trumpet blast
A mighty shout
Prepare the battle without
A trash can's victory
About to repeal, set them free

Keep not thy tongue
Run Church, run!

~

April 24, 2018
DISTANCE FROM THE STAIN

Distance from the stain
Calls for repentance
Change, change, change
Run oh sinner—hear the call:
CHRIST JESUS saves us all.

Tabernacle choir???
What do I hear?
Standing ovation?
Cheer, cheer!

~

April - May, 2018
THE BATTLE OF JERICHO
{Song sing to tune of Joshua fought the battle of Jericho}

Joshua fought *the battle of Jericho*
Jericho, Jericho
With this we know
We fight Roe
We fight Roe
With this we do know
Roe will come tumbling down
A fortress, a stronghold
But a mighty GOD we do know
Just as did Jericho
The walls come a tumbling down

~

MARCH FOR THIS OR THAT

You'll march for this
You'll march for that.
You'll march for a dollar bill.
Will you march for that
which kills?

~

April 29 2018
A ROYAL FLUSH

A royal flush
A command
GOD'S gon'na open HIS hand
Calling Christians
Lay down your life
Pick up your armor
Run for a light
Begin to wield a sword
Run for THE LORD

God is flushing out the system commanding us to pray, speak truth and stop Abortion!

~

March 13, 2018
OKLAHOMA REPEALS

Oklahoma *repeals* Abortion Law
Evil killing of children will fall

[1]Midterm exam,
Need to plan, plan, plan

Crossing a river
A Word to deliver

MENE, MENE, TEKEL, UPHARSIN

A shout to arise
Cries to the skies

[2]Mountaintop birthed
Revealing more Earth

[3]Northern Hemisphere

[1]*Nov elections*
[2]*Hawaiian volcano*
[3]*referring to ring of fire*

~

December 7, 2018
ALASKA

What's up with Alaska?
Hear their cry?
I'm not finished say I
Reach out their hand
A blessing they shall cry
Huffing and puffing, blow the house down
Shiver me timbers that won't be found?
Atomic blast? They threaten at last?
Will be for naught, they shall be taught
Temperance dog sleds
Number them instead.

Ethnic religious purity resolved
Reckoned all national call
Hear, hear I say again

Look not at the color of thy skin
Red was shed for one and all
A blessing now, hear MY call

America stay the course
This hour witches' power turns sour
Burdensome relief, a new belief
Cast thy care, *cannabis* rare, hovers there!

Christian onslaught will be taught
Peanut farmer, your sons be.
Standing soon next to me

Oklahoma churches rise
Purity they don't despise
Proof given ME they see
GOD'S people on TV.

Johnny Cash show
It shall flow
Charlie Pride they shall hide,

Governor of the state
Prophesy again, again doesn't mean they will win
Texas, Arizona, Missouri and the rest
Will be put to the test.

Gabriel now does thy horn blow
Many, many, time to go!

Tragedy; came to watch it on T.V.
Sons and daughters cry for waters
Local channels all a scramble.

Let's go home: camp alone

Veggie Tales hits the spot
Rotten fruit it is not

Many fossils of the apostles
Tribesmen came, what a shame
College degree, reckless decree

Cartoons soon fills the room
Jonah's whale rings a bell!
Noah's ark soon departs!

Easy street soon complete
Africa dark, soon depart
Finish what you start

Hip-huggers and bell-bottoms
Shaggy hair and fool's Sodom!
Grace to see reversal of these.

~

September 3, 2018
EZEKIEL'S MESSAGE

Ezekiel
I sent you a message, I gave you a dream,
You had a vision
What more needs, it seems
WHEEL WITHIN WHEEL
Staircase to HEAVEN

Falling stars, racing lessons

Blood moons, high tides,
Tsunamis, trees fried
Bodies a bloat
No need now to send a boat
Earthquakes many,
Choosing any
Which *sign* now do I send?
Wake up, wake up, wake up,
My friend?
Captain, captain, captain, falling stars
For I'M about this world to jar
The seas will roar,
The mountains explode,
On to ME only
Should you hold.

~

September 3, 2018
EZEKIEL'S WARNING FROM GOD
{Prophetic}

Ezekiel heard the call
On his face he did fall.
Trying times hc did live,
Sharing happenings about to give.
Warnings, dreams about to transpire,
Were brought about from A HIGHER POWER

Fun times? No!
A shout about
What's going without
Religion says, fear not!
I say
—WARNING!—
Hot spot
—HIGH RED ALERT!—
Crimson tide about to hit this Earth.

~

November 19, 2018
JUNIPER

Mirror, mirror on the wall
Crazy things begin to fall
[1]Juniper arises as a nation despises
The demise of closing tiny eyes

Capitalization reduces the abomination.
Evil, wicked, standing go
Kingdom come, JESUS knows

Monster [scary] we will see,
Showing up quite rapidly!
Tender matches, races away
A puff of smoke as childish play.
Fever pitched win, win!
[2]No worries about {Trump} then

Let MY people go
Abruptly I will show
Exactly how I treated
Pharoah
Recompense makes no sense?
[3]Vengeance is MINE
HE says all the time

[1]*Juniper arises as a nation despises and continues in her rebellion to God's judgements; they refuse to let go of the sacrilege of abortion. Just like they replaced the Sycamore with a Cedar tree after the Twin Towers fell on 9/11/2001.*

[2]*At the time of the writing of this book, New York passes a bill to take abortion out of the penal code and move it into the Health Code.*

Thus, making it legal to abort babies up to the point of birth (and beyond)—thereby New York state is literally shaking its fist in utter rebellion in the face of Washington, President Trump, and The Holy GOD of the Bible.

[3]*Romans 2:4-6 NLT*
4 Don't you see how wonderfully kind, tolerant, and patient God is with you? Does this mean nothing to you? Can't you see that his kindness is intended to turn you from your sin?

5 But because you are stubborn and refuse to turn from your sin, you are storing up terrible punishment for yourself. For a day of anger is coming, when God's righteous judgment will be revealed.

6 He will judge everyone according to what they've done.

~

March 10, 2018
ARK OF THE COVENANT
{Prophetic}

Soon the world
Will know I exist
The ark of MY covenant
Will come to rest
In Jerusalem again

Oh LORD what have we found
As we opened the ground

On our faces we fall
One and all

For MY glory is there
No one dare compare

*It is the belief of the author that Ron Wyatt accurately told
of His discovery. {See archives of Ron Wyatt Discoveries}*

~

May 24, 2018
TRIFECTA

Justice
Travesty
Disappearing
Choking, damaged, broken
Verily, verily I say unto thee
I chose to die upon the tree
The children, babies, little ones
Forbid them not to me to come
Catholic grave mistake
Indoctrination, they do make
Bread of life
Moving out
Anchored stout
Groping hoping
Children yoking
Grandchildren
Voiceless
Life shorted—Aborted
Wesleyan
Kicking alive
Shouting
I survived
A beautiful
Surprise

~

April 17, 2018

MORNINGS ON THE HORIZONS

Mornings on the horizons
Hugging children, not despising
Tousled heads, and little feet
Running with open arms to greet
Oh boy my daddy, he's coming home.
Couches covered in toys, and *Sunday funnies*
Cluttered hallways, getting ready for Mondays
Church in a minute
Got to rush, we'll be in it.
Coming home to Sunday dinner
Eating chicken, it's a winner!
Making up a backyard team;
Gon'na win, my turn, I sing
Trooping into house at night,
Running baths, and turning lights.
PJ's on, ready for bed.
Did I say my prayers instead?
No, I forgot! Sliding out upon the rug
Folding hands, my pillow hug.
Please dear JESUS remember me?
I'm the one who came to be
Abortion stopped so I came in
Thank YOU JESUS
YOU are my FRIEND!!!

~

HURRY! HURRY!
{Prophetic}

Hurry! Hurry! Morbidity rate,
Getting closer it's now too late
Thunder now I hear on the horizon
Rumblings now underground arising

Feeling the ire
Of a holy GOD'S fire
Toil, toil, toil, and trouble
Witches' brew start to bubble?

No, it's a full plate
Of the *blood sacrifice* of the children
It's now too late!
Double recompense
Of the blood as the earth does vent.
Erupting and spewing out
Ankle deep rivers of fire, you will shout

Hearken not, to MY WORD
Spewing you out, you now have heard
BOOM! BOOM! The sacrifice
Double barrel, I won't think twice
I won't apologize, analyze, or disguise
As I open-up the skies
To give rise for your recompense
Heaven or Hell?

It came from whence North, South, East, or West
North MY children say best
MY actions louder than words
Now you have heard

Blood sacrifice?
You might wanna think twice.

~

April 21, 2018
BELSHAZZAR

Belshazzar saw the writing
On the wall;
So, scared his knees
Knocked, about to fall.

He cared not, the others shared not.
Only truth will help me here,
These words did not casually appear.
Decode this for me please,
So, I can stop my trembling knees.

Bring me the brightest in the land
To tell me about this hand!
Only Daniel in THE BOOK
(Chapter 5)
Could decipher the words to the wise.

Be afraid oh, my king

For weighed and wanted
Justice has seen.
Weighed and balanced
By MY WORD,
You MY judgement now have heard.

~

October 21, 2018
DECEMBER REMEMBERS
{Prophetic}

December remembers
November's embers
Mexico's antics produces frantics
Jumping the stage begins the rage
A tinder box November rocks
Rumbling deep within the earth
Giving way about to birth
Chances call for us all
Mystery changes believers ranges
Putin scoot'in, believer's root'in
Parliament raises to vent
Syracuse brings big news
Actors, reactors, factors, chapters
Stages, rages, hate filled pages
Believers receive Genesis relieved
Lucky, lucky in Kentucky
Arkansas wins it all

The whips crush rebellion's stuff
Guiding stages of refugee age
Foreigners rage
Jackie Robinson time; arise, shine
Playball!
Fever pitched it comes to call
Socrate's theocracy

~

January 23, 2019
FEAR OF GOD?

Fear of GOD?
Where America do we trod?
Murder in New York town,
Proudly hailed at the sound.
Sea to shining sea?
Oh, America!
—Return quickly on thy knees.
About to come tumbling down;
Tower of babble crashing to the ground.
Humble not thyself? I say,
—Fear THE LORD—
For great humbling is on the way!

~

January, 2019
LABRESKA'S POINT

While we weep for our cancerous loved ones to be healed
The destiny of the world is being *altered*
by *the babies we kill.*
Where an *innocent* child's *blood* is being shed
We go our own ways, and turn our heads
But there is no mercy shown
As we spare not, and kill our own.
For God's great love is open to all
Yet *the murdered unborn* aren't allowed to hear His call
60 Million aborted, does that turn your head?
Roll that over in your head; in fear and dread.
For even an 18 yr. old can see with clear eyes,
The generation to come must not be despised.
For we are the ones who must give rise
To hear these little babies' cries.

~

FROM THE HOLY ONE

A fiery dearth, a flame sent to the earth
Just like in *the days of Jonah*;
Sent to warn the people of Ninevah.
A fiery wind will soon descend;

Bringing decisions to an end.
Repent and be quick about it, for the heavens do shout it.
THE LORD OF HOST is HIS NAME
Believe on HIM and there will be great gain.
Turning away from your sin, is where it does all begin.
Forgiveness belongs to ME
You will know this and you will see
For I THE LORD OF HOST am great to he
Who does call upon MY NAME.
There is no other who can claim
The sea, the land and the heavens,
Oh by the way, the universe too
I spoke into existence long before you!
Are you ready for this, can your mere mind understand
I have a way and MY plan is MY plan
Foolishness is bound in the heart of man
But the rod of correction can uproot this evil plan.
Brace yourselves and get ready
I AM the only thing that is steady
I AM THE ROCK that does not roll
I AM about to unfold this show.
So, enter in and *save your soul.*

THE GOOD NEWS

~

GOOD NEWS—YOU CAN BE FREE!

We must understand: *For everyone has sinned; we all fall short of God's glorious standard. - (Ro 3:23 NLT)*

The GOOD NEWS is, God in His great wisdom and love for humanity has designed a SALVATION plan through His Son JESUS, wherein we can be forgiven, and restored (in our heart, mind and emotions).

FACT: *For the wages of sin is death, but the free gift of God is eternal life through Christ Jesus our Lord. - (Ro 6:23 NLT)*

But God commendeth his love toward us, in that, while we were yet sinners, [JESUS] Christ died for us. - (Ro 5:8 NLT)

HOPE: This plan is so perfect, so complete, that it brings human beings back into close fellowship with God Himself. We become His children and HE becomes OUR FATHER; and as children of God we are guaranteed to escape the judgements soon to come on this old world. And one day we will spend all of eternity with Him in Heaven.

LOVE: *"For God loved the world so much that he gave his one and only Son, so that everyone who believes in him will not perish but have eternal life." - (Jo 3:16 NLT)*

IF YOU BELIEVE JESUS died and rose alive again to make this possible? Just say a simple prayer (out loud): *"Jesus I believe you died for me, and that You are alive now* *forever. I believe You are the only Savior for mankind—please save me, be my Lord for the rest of my life."*

GUARANTEE: *For "Everyone who calls on the name of the LORD will be saved." - (Ro 10:13 NLT)*

A FUTURE: *But now being made free from sin, and become servants to God, ye have your fruit [motive and actions] unto holiness, and the end everlasting life. - (Ro 6:22 KJV)*

NEW IDENTITY: You are now a Christian (a born-again [saved] follower of Christ), get a Bible and read some of it daily, find a good church and attend often, pray everyday.

~

September 23, 2018
JESUS LOVES THE LITTLE CHILDREN

JESUS loves the little children
All the children of the world.
A fool learns not to blaspheme
By the correction he has seen.

Steady, sturdy as she goes
Is the light though the wind blows.
Nature tells us through a study stream
Mighty rivers form from its mean.

Kingdoms come and kingdoms go
But CHRIST will return, this we know.

Prophets warn of impending doom
Mass confusion, fear, and gloom.

Our HEAVENLY FATHER I hear say
Put forth thy hand, be healed today.
A child innocent, pure and sweet
To see THE MASTER we must like him, compete.

Harvest time is now here
But judgement is all I hear.
Report for duty I hear THE MASTER say
Walk MY path, stay MY way.

Hunger and thirst for righteousness
Ankle deep, shed thy sleep, cry for holiness.
Enter a new time, Church of MINE
Wet behind the ears? Wonders will appear.

Discernment? Audible voices?
Look not to the left or right
The harvest is here—the fields are ripe!
Red or yellow, black, brown or white
Color blind is MY SPIRIT sight!

~

September 23, 2018
LIGHT THE TENDER

Light the tender, strike up the coal.
Time for America to know.

Burning fire of desire
Fast or slow?
Time for revival in MINE America.
Winds of revival, spirit of change
Return to America, sweep over her soul again.
Across this nation, let them be chasin'
A love of THE FATHER
So deep
It'll make men weep.
Let them yearn
For true joy to return.
Rocked by the cradle
Of men who are able.
Silver spoon removed
Giving faith room.
Growth, *a new chapter*
Not just looking for the rapture.
Church eyes skyward, walking on higher.
Things of this world cast away
Mustering obedience to pray.
Across the hallowed halls
Let true religion call
[1]*James 1:27*
Bring down HEAVEN.
America, America will ye be
A burning light once again for ME?

[1]*Pure religion and undefiled before God and the Father is this, to visit the fatherless, and widows in their affliction, and to keep himself unspotted from the world. James 1:27 KJV*

~

July, 2018
JESUS, JESUS

YOU had a choice
To die on that tree, YOU did not rejoice.
To sacrifice a SAVIOR'S LIFE
YOU did some praying
YOU had to think twice
For the joy [1]set before YOU
YOU paid the price
YOU beat the devil
But YOU sacrificed.
To overcome him, YOU had to decide
Obedience to death to die.
A miracle we did see
When YOUR WILL was laid down in Gethsemane
For the joy set before YOU
YOU counted the cost.
YOU knew disobedience,
To humanity would be lost
But that was not why YOU chose to obey
For I believe it was to hear THE FATHER say
Well done MY SON
Enter YOUR reward today.

[1]*For the joy that was set before Him, he endured the cross, despising shame and hath set down at the right hand of the throne of God. - Hebrews 12:2 KJV*

~

November, 2018
RAW COURAGE

Raw courage, beautiful tide
Dancing dreams of MY Bride.
Actors staging all the hope
Rebellion aging a long rope.
Given enough it will seem
in the end a hangman's dream.
Gallows waiting for MY Bride?
Hide and watch; Haman's hide.
Jezebel swinging on the rope,
No longer leaning on the lies she wrote.
Fearful, tearful, the country watches,
Gleeful the opposition opts.
A counterfeit report
A challenging retort.
Captain! captain!
True *Veggie Tales*,
Written in form of *witches' spells*.
Liar, liar pants on fire!
Vengeance is MINE sayeth
THE LORD
They will learn MY WORD to not abhor!
Dust off thy boots hang up thy clothes
Mystery this winter I will expose!

~

September 16, 2018
ALL CREATION YEARS

Biblical complaints, HIGHER POWER
Rotten fruit, a tower
Jezebel spirit, live and learn
Foolish rebellion, you spurn
Carbon copy as before
Live and let live, no more
Steady as she goes, it fits
Sees them thru a pit
A wall, *valley of dry bones*
A people coming home
Ancient sacrifice, burial that's nice
Crystal sea, transport me
Patience, a fruit
Lesson, take root
Vengeance not mine, only divine
Atkins you ask, declare a fast
Cannabis please, beautiful leaves?
HOLY SPIRIT *fire* instead of these,
Apocalyptic times, reason for these rhymes
All creation yearns, for YESHUA'S return
Hold thy tongue not
Preach on the spot.

These are situations and problems, the Church and the world faces today. Each one has an answer. Each answer is found in the Word of God.

There are many things happening in the world today that are identical to the days of rebellion during the time of Queen Jezebel's Reign. In the church world God is calling His people out of the attitude of live and let live, into the truth.

We must stand against the evil of our day, and not be ashamed of The Gospel of Jesus Christ. God says to love what HE loves and hate what HE hates. Speak out! Stand! Declare the truth!

We are a peculiar people called to show forth the praises of Him who hath called us out of darkness into HIS marvelous light. We are the light of the world and the salt of the earth! We must Proclaim the truth to a desperate and dying world.

Abortion is innocent blood sacrifice this is an ancient practice. In America we don't even bother to bury our sacrificed children. We dump them in landfills and grind their body parts to use for face creams to keep us looking youthful and nice. And yes, we, the Church are guilty of this every time we buy that jar of face cream. Answer? Stop! Cry aloud!

Crystal Sea transport me; JESUS is THE PRINCE of PEACE

Marijuana to soothe us, instead turn to God's Spirit.

Hunting for the next new diet fad to solve our growing obesity problem? A fast, problem solved, and money saved.

The Church is turning to the world for the answers and God is saying the true Church must come out and turn to His Word and Him for the answers to every problem we face.

We must show the world what we got; that by actions and a mouth only—not.

The Spirit of the Living God has the answer to these problems—The Good News

If any of you lack wisdom, let him ask God and He will give it to you; He will not rebuke you for asking. (James 1:5 NLT)

~

September 23, 2018
STEADY AS SHE GOES

Steady, steady, steady as she goes
For here I hear what no one else knows
So as the story unfolds
Rapture ready I am told
Better to be than to hit my knees
When it's too late
But right with JESUS is all it takes
Loving HIM.
Is where it all begins

~

March 2, 2018
THE GREATEST GENERATION

The greatest generation
Children of the great depression

Surrounded by all this wisdom
Oh LORD how we will miss them!
Bowers of love
Staunch defenders of
The blood
Being wise
THE LORD always before their eyes.
Brave and bold
Going on we are told
No matter what, they questioned sin a lot.
Obeying not evil men
They refused, so they win.
Bending or breaking for a whim
You won't find it in them.
Now they are standing in a blaze of glory
For in their lives, they lived
The old, old story

∾

March 3, 2018

JOY BELL HAS RUNG

Leap for joy, MY wonderous faith
Jump for joy, don't be late
Shout for joy alive and behold

Joy comes because YOU reign
Washed by love's blood stain

Repent and cry aloud
JESUS is coming do it proud

Joy can be seen everywhere
Even from birds in the air

Pick up your pencil, go for the prize
Go for the gold, don't despise

Preach THE GOSPEL to the poor and thin
Preach THE GOSPEL, pour it in.

Alive you shall stand, join the call
Baptized in fire, show love to all

Love *Isaiah 60*
Gives the call
Tell GOOD NEWS to them all
Report what THE LORD has done
How *the joy bell* has rung!

∽

October, 2018
RAW REMNANT WARRIORS

A different breed.
A sacrificial offering.
Poured out for a need.
Standing on a battlefield
Glory coming from a cloud, that's real!
Courses set for the hour.

Great raw remnant power!
Never falling by the side,
Watching, waiting for victor's ride.
A sealed generation knowing this hour
Marching orders for an enemy to devour
In the shadow of THE MOST HIGH
Exploding brilliant is MY Bride.

~

JOHN 3:16—THE GOOD NEWS

Trouncing and traipsing through this world,
A new generation toward eternity does hurl
Without THE GOSPEL it seems
This brings us to:
[1]John 3:16
—GOOD NEWS—
*How lovely on the mountain are the feet of them that
bring good news. (Isaiah 52:7)*

*[1]For God so loved the world, that he gave his only begotten
Son, that whosoever believeth in him should not perish, but
have everlasting life. (John 3:16 KJV)*

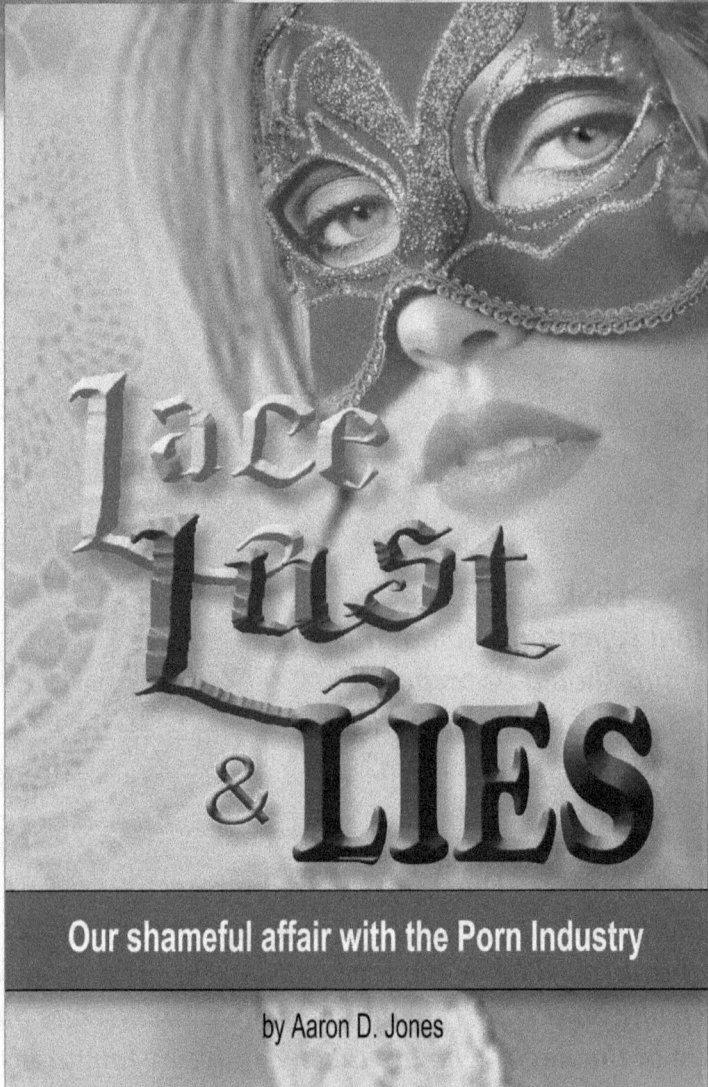

www.ingramcontent.com/pod-product-compliance
Lightning Source LLC
Chambersburg PA
CBHW060046100426
42742CB00014B/2721